OVERBOARD!

AND OTHER CANALLING MISHAPS

Hadleigh Court

OVERBOARD!

AND OTHER CANALLING MISHAPS

OR

CANAL CRUISING WITH 'L' PLATES

OR

UP THE CUT WITHOUT A CLUE

JOHN COOK

With illustrations by Tony Forbes

Hadleigh Court

Published by Hadleigh Court Books
The Ridgeway, Bristol, BS10 7DG.

ISBN - 978-0-9555087-0-7

The paper used in this book is sourced from a fully managed forestry system and is oxygen rather than chemically bleached.

Printed by The Woodside Press Ltd., Bristol, UK.

DEDICATION

For Bill and Selina who persuaded me to take up
canal cruising, little realizing quite how
much it would change my life.

Contents

Preface

"When we were directly opposite, the man at the bows fell in! One moment he was holding a rope with one hand and waving and smiling, the next he was dropping vertically into about five feet of water. As he pulled himself out we tried tactfully to look the other way for there are few things more embarrassing than a ducking."
[**WATER BYWAYS** by David E. Owen.]

The expression 'to go overboard' doesn't only mean to fall off a boat into the water – although this is a common enough experience – but has the more long term meaning of 'fall for', 'fall in love with', 'lose control', etc. Boats and boating, whatever the water, have a fascination many of us are helpless to resist.

This book is written with the 'first time hirer' particularly in mind. That was how most of us got our first taste of ditchcrawling and lockwheeling and caught the canal bug.

So, whether you are afloat or on dry land, put your feet up for a good read and laugh all the way, as you fall overboard.

John Cook.
The Moorings,
The Happy Boater Inn,
Somewhere-up-the-cut.

1 *Why do it?*

"What? cried the Rat, open mouthed:
"Never been in a – you never – well, I –
What have you been doing then?"
[**The Wind in the Willows** by Kenneth Graham.]

PERHAPS it's because we live on an island and our national heroes include the likes of the one-eyed, one-armed Admiral Nelson, putting that famous telescope to his blind eye and commenting for posterity "I see no ships!" and that demon bowler, Francis Drake, quipping "Methinks it were a merry jape to sail over to Spain and singe the King's beard." or words to that effect. Then again, maybe it's Ridgeway and Blyth we should blame for popularizing extreme rowing, or more recently those fearless solo yacht-girls Tracey Edwards, Ellen MacArthur and Dee Caffari for giving boating such a high profile. Why, even fourteen-year-olds are at it now!

Every other week there's a news item of some fearless Brit. setting off on a trans-oceanic sailing or rowing trip in a twenty-footer he knocked up over a few weekends in his back garden. These are usually followed weeks – or in some cases only hours – after they set out by the story of how they had to be rescued by the emergency services.

It seems that some of us just can't help ourselves! Polite people call it 'boating madness', others describe our affliction in more salty language, but to no avail. Once caught, this fascination with all things *boaty* seems impossible to ignore. If it happens to you the only answer is to reorganize your life to fit in as much boating as possible, and enjoy every minute of it.

While the most deranged sufferers are infected so badly they rush out and buy a boat, more cautious victims tend to start off with taking boat trips, rowing, punting and sailing or booking a holiday cruising in the Med or the Caribbean or around Birmingham. Yes, boating can take many forms and you may have to experiment a bit until you realize which is the right one for you.

Up to the age of ten I thought I'd like to 'go to sea' when I grew up. Then one year we went to Wales for our summer holiday. My father (whose only previous claim to boating fame was to heave an anchor over the side without checking to see if there was any rope tied to it) took me on a trip along the coast in an elderly open wooden fishing boat, *Bay Tripper*. The outward leg of what was supposed to be a one hour outing passed without incident, although the blue sky beneath which we boarded gradually turned grey and the rising wind brought the two dozen passengers out in goose bumps.

When the Captain was about to turn round to head back, the ancient engine coughed and wheezed and abruptly died. It was then I realised this cruise was not going to be quite as advertised. With the waves slopping noisily against the planking, increasingly splashing the shirt-sleeved passengers, the mood on board felt similar to our rather inadequate vessel; less than buoyant.

Nobody spoke as our bearded skipper in his battered cap and waders, removed the cover from the engine housing and peered at the sizzling mass of hot metal. "Use the oars to keep her head-on." he instructed his mate, a twiggy youth, who since helping us clamber aboard had been trying to make himself sick smoking Woodbines. Now, perhaps sensing his own preservation might depend on it, the sluggish mate sprang into action.

The sea, which had become a bit too playful, chose not to crush our cockleshell on the rocky shore but to drag us away from it. While our skipper exercised his engineering know-how to the limit, his mate struggled to turn *Bay Tripper*. Unfortunately he bent not just his back but also both the oars and, with an alarming 'crack', one of them suddenly snapped in half. Sailing wasn't an option as the wooden stump, between the engine and bow masquerading as a mast, was barely tall enough to fly a handkerchief-sized 'skull and crossbones'.

If anyone was saying prayers at this stage, mercifully, they did so silently. "Will we all be drownded?" a child near me asked. There was an agonising pause before first one and then every adult chimed in with variations of "Of course not."; "We'll be alright." and "There's nothing to worry about.". All good 'stiff-upper-lip' stuff.

If I'd been sitting closer to our muttering skipper, still on his knees tinkering with the unco-operative engine, I'd have learned some choice Welsh expletives as the boat wallowed pathetically and, with the mist closing in, the coast quickly disappeared from sight.

After wiping his oily hands on a scrap of cloth, the skipper tried the ignition again and this time the engine spluttered back into life. "Just a bit of dirt in the fuel pipe." he advised a relieved audience. We all anxiously listened to every grumble and chunter of the elderly motor, but somehow it kept running.

We didn't know it at the time, but a sizeable crowd of the passengers' nearest and dearest had gathered on the quay where concern for our safety was growing with every passing minute. On board *Bay Tripper* spray began breaking over the stern and the water previously sploshing and gurgling around the bilges could be felt massaging our feet. With the mounting waves, the old engine was

Our skipper exercised his engineering know-how to the limit

finding it hard work and occasionally missed a beat; each time, I imagine every heart on board did the same.

The light was fading and our bare arms were turning blue before someone on shore sighted our boat. Through the mist and spray we could just make out the huddle of figures impotently waving at us. As they gradually grew larger and the old boat huffed and puffed her way inshore, my father murmured to me "I hope your mother hasn't been worried."

No-one gave *Bay Tripper*'s skipper any credit or thanks for bringing us back safely, as, helped by a wall of grabbing arms, we all scrambled off the vessel as fast as any young men ever left a bar at the approach of the dreaded Press Gang. It felt so good to be back on solid ground.

The results of this exploit – after a tear-stained hug from my mother – were, in chronological order:

(i) My father was made to promise never to take me out on such a trip again;

(ii) We missed our tea; and

(iii) I decided very definitely **not** to put my name down for the Royal Navy.

It was only years later, when I was introduced to cruising on the successors to James Brindley's 'stinking ditch', the canals, that I discovered the sort of boating I could fall for. From that day I became addicted and over the years my family has come to accept that this is one of those weird conditions for which there is no cure.

Whether your urge to go boating is inspired by reading *Swallows and Amazons* or *Treasure Island* as a child, one of those holiday programmes on TV, or a magazine article, for a week or two you can be captain of your own narrow boat and live out your fantasies. You can even dress up as a pirate if you want and hobble around on one leg with a parrot on your shoulder muttering "Aha, Jim lad!" and nobody will mind. They will probably think you've been bending your elbow too much, or spent too long in the sun, but they won't mind.

You don't need to ask someone who owns a boat to lend it to you – it's best not to anyway, they'd expect it back in one piece. Fortunately there are plenty of trusting hire companies on the canals that – in return for your cash – will, almost unbelievably, let you loose with a craft worth several times the price of a new family saloon, without you taking a driving test, providing evidence of sanity or having any previous boating experience. All you need are a few people brave enough to go with you.

2 *Taking the plunge.*

"Our fleet ranges from quality boats to more basic types."
[**Hire Company Brochure**.]

SOME out-of-date killjoys may still imagine the canals are linear cesspools along which grimy boats are worked by even grimier bargees through smoke-blackened suburbs of the industrial Midlands. The scene is very different today, and as for the boats you can hire, they are almost as sparkling as those featured in the hire companies' brochures.

Married hirers may be expected to accompany their spouse, however he or she may not share your enthusiasm to 'spend a week in a floating caravan', and you may need to negotiate their co-operation with a sweetener; maybe letting them choose your next holiday, agreeing to your in-laws coming for Christmas or replacing your old box with a plasma TV. Never mind, it will be worth it, I hope.

Canal holidays are ideal for families – well, that's what all the hire firms claim in their literature. Having children or pets (or a collection of both) shouldn't prevent anyone choosing a boating holiday. Although you might prefer to leave them at home in the care of a neighbour, most parents will feel that their children at least ought to come with them, and some may insist on taking their dog, cat, budgie, hamster, ferret or mina bird as well.

As for children, they are never too young to start. Sarah, my eldest daughter, went on her first boating holiday when she was only three weeks old, an ideal age. Once babies become mobile they're more accident-prone and toddlers have to be watched all the time, otherwise they tend to fall in the canal. But, considering all the other horrors and degrading activities parents subject their offspring to in the course of growing up, there seems no reason to exclude a boating holiday from their catalogue of learning experiences.

One economical option is to share a large boat with another family. That way you're able to spread the cost and at the same time the children will have instant friends to play, argue and fight with – just like their parents.

For singles, if your invitation to spend a week afloat is rejected with replies such as "Boating?!!", "With *you*?!!!" or "I'd rather spend a fortnight visiting crematoria!" don't let this dent your enthusiasm. Tell yourself "These ignoramuses don't know what they'll be missing!"; and that's the truth. Hopefully your next attempts will be more successful. Plenty of people 'have thought about a boating holiday'. You just have to track some down and get them to commit to dates. Many such arrangements must have been reached at the end of an evening down the pub.

I have to both thank and blame my Father-in-law, Bill. It was back in the Seventies that he suggested the idea of exploring the Llangollen Canal. I must have had a glass or two when I agreed to book a boat and to spend a week afloat with him and my wife, Selina, plus my sister, Jillie, her husband, Max, and their three-month-old baby, Guy. Not knowing the ropes, I scoured the weekend papers for adverts and got half a dozen hire companies to send me their details. Within the week we were all committed.

Back in those days the choices were a lot simpler. There was no question of picking a boat with colour TV, a microwave and central heating. You were pleased to get bunks for everyone with sleeping bags, some form of toilet and a cooker. Today making your choice is much harder, but then modern boats are a lot more comfortable.

Hire boat operators even have their own websites nowadays, so (apart from technophobes, who should stick to the printed brochures) finding details of possible companies should be no problem. Choosing the right company and the best boat, that's a different story.

In recent years hire boat companies have started putting what they call 'full size' fixed double beds on their boats, because "this is what our customers have demanded". This suggests that some hirers are more interested in mattress dancing than actually cruising. If you plump for this luxury don't expect the bed to be very wide, but do expect it to turn into a popular dumping ground for everybody's kit throughout your trip.

You'll soon realize that prices vary from budget to de luxe. **Splendid Cruisers'** boats are obviously far more luxuriously equipped than your home and beyond all but the deepest pocket. At the other end of the scale is **Brown's Budget Boat Co.** They are definitely more affordable, indeed compared to **Pretty Narrowboats Ltd.**, **The Blissful Boating Company**, **Faraway Boats**, **Croeso Cruisers** and **Dawn Cruisers (Nether Itchingden) Ltd.**, their prices are below rock bottom. Surely there must be some catch!

You may decide (unless you're Welsh) that **Croeso Cruisers** is a non-starter, with boats called *Ynysbwllog*, *Pontcysyllte, Ynysangarad* and *Ystralgynlais,* you'll never even be able to pronounce them! Equally, the thought of spending a week on *Pretty Doreen*, *Pretty Mabel* or *Pretty Ursula* may strike some members of your party as pretty embarrassing, pretty pathetic and pretty naff.

Like all material designed to sell something, hire company brochures are written in code. To help you understand them here are some common phrases and their ***real*** meanings.

Popular Layout:.....Unchanged for the last twenty years.
Quiet engine:.....It may vibrate a lot, but it's not so noisy as some boats.
Co-ordinated decor::.....Everything is brown.
Maximum privacy: .....You can draw a curtain across between the cabins.
Open plan layout:......You can move the table and chairs.
Economical on fuel:.....We charge you for a full tank of diesel, but you won't use more than half.
Large well at front:.....Somewhere handy to put Granny.
Plenty of space for everyone: Standing room only.
Pets welcome:.....Our boats don't have carpets.

Some other examples of *'brochurese'* you'll find include the following:'*compact*'; this is probably the most accurate and truthful description in any hire company's bumph: *'spacious'*; which of course means 'in comparison to our compact model'; *'Ideally suited to the larger group'* is holiday sales jargon for 'This boat is a miracle of shoe-horning a quart into a pint pot and may be a bit dented'; while *'Excellent value for money'*; is probably the most meaningless expression ever concocted, translating as anything from 'This boat cost a lot to fit out and we must recover our outlay as fast as possible' down to 'If you pay the lowest prices, what can you expect!'

It isn't only the brochure's words that need careful interpretation, all those colourful photos are designed to mislead as much as to inform would-be hirers. The people responsible for producing them must work to a strict set of guidelines. I imagine those for the photographer would look something like this:

1.) No hint must ever appear of rain or wind. On our boats it is always very sunny.

2.) All camera angles must emphasize the spaciousness of each craft.

3.) Interior shots should, wherever possible, be taken from outside the boat.

4.) The boats should preferably be shown empty. If models are used they must be slim, tanned, impeccably groomed and less than five feet four inches tall.
5.) The number of models appearing in any shot should never exceed half the number of persons the boat can sleep.
6.) No clutter (including boating equipment) should be visible. The only exception being the inclusion of one garment or towel artistically placed for maximum effect.
7.) Every surface must be spotless and shining, so the entire boat will look as though a squad of cleaners have spent several hours cleaning it. (This, of course, is exactly what they did before the photoshoot.)

Eventually you succeed in narrowing your options down to Faraway Boats, The Blissful Boating Company and Dawn Cruisers (Nether Itchingden) Ltd. If names count for anything then Faraway Boats have a definite edge with *Hawaii*, *Tahiti* and *Bali,* but, unfortunately, their hire base is a bit far away too. Several hours of searching your road maps of the Midlands reveals where the minute hamlet of Nether Itchingden is hiding and that it will take about the same time to drive to the Blissful Boating Co. It's a tricky choice for the novice hirer, good luck!

Your final decision may depend on weeks of painstaking scrutiny of every detail or the quicker method of tossing a coin. Then again, by the time you try to book it, the boat you were after may no longer be available. Do not faint when you calculate how much this holiday is going to cost. You could probably fly off to the Spanish 'costas' for two weeks for less, but what's the attraction of loafing around in the sun for days on end when you could be messing about on a boat in England? Perhaps that is a question that can only be answered after it is all over.

Once the booking is made, don't worry about what you've let yourself (and all the rest of your party) in for. Think positive. Spend the intervening weeks plundering your local library for 'how to' books on inland boating, quick and easy cooking and staying calm in a crisis, also buy some sun lotion and look out your waterproof clothing.

Let's hope that nobody drops out, you all remain on speaking terms, that you haven't selected the wettest week of the year and your boat lives up to the brochure description. One thing that can be predicted with some confidence is that your holiday afloat will be an experience you will never forget.

3 *Love at first sight?*

"For most people there is inevitably a certain amount of anxiety associated with managing a boat for the first time."
[**The Inland Navigator** by Bryan Marsh.]

AFTER weeks of waiting, the morning of your holiday dawns. Despite having to turn back for forgotten items such as the directions on how to find the hire base, some young person's favourite toy and some not-so-young person's spare false teeth, you and your party reach the boatyard on the right date. Now the enormity of your responsibility may really hit you. If anything goes wrong in the next week it is bound to be blamed on you. Already you can anticipate the cries of "It was your stupid idea.", "I'd never have come if you hadn't talked me into it." and "I should have known any holiday organised by you would be a disaster!" Now it is too late, you can only fight down your fears, tell everyone it's going to be a great week and hope that you will get the hang of all the steering and locks and manage to return the boat in one piece and on time.

Amid the chaotic scurry of other hirers emptying their cars and carting cases and armfuls of supplies to the nearby line of boats, a scruffy man in oil-stained overalls directs you to Blissful Boats' office. Here you're handed the keys and told that Gary will be along soon to take you through the briefing. So it's back to the car to start lugging everything in it over to your home for the next seven days: *Blissful Daze*, (Dawn Cruisers' boats weren't such a nice colour.)

To get on board your boat you may have to clamber over several others, each swarming with eager children and ambivalent adults carrying innumerable cases and boxes. Alternatively, you may be lucky and find *Blissful Daze* moored stern on to the wharf. So all that your crew need to do is haul themselves (and of course all their luggage and supplies) over the stern rail. This is when you will wish (and not for the last time on your trip) that the rear end of your boat was straight instead of the awkward rounded shape she is. If half your collection of canalling innocents can't even reach the back deck, drop the groceries into the canal or injure themselves in their attempts to get on board, the complaints may begin straight away.

As you will all soon learn, canal boats have a few snares for the unwary. For instance there's the sliding roof hatch, which will try to trap everyone's fingers, and below this, immediately inside the back doors lurk a short steep flight of narrow steps that will do their best to trip each of you up all week.

Loading all your gear on board will be complicated as it is virtually impossible for two people to pass each other. Anyone carrying a case or box of provisions will need to hold in their stomach while simultaneously twisting sideways. The not-so-slim members of your crew will soon find themselves wedged in the narrow corridor, but it would be cruel to leave them behind for such a simple shortcoming. If the rest of your crew can't manage, you may have to hump all the luggage on board yourself, even if you acquire a hernia in the process. Just take care not to fall down those steps.

Many novices think the most important thing on their first day is to successfully get the boat out of the boatyard. They are totally mistaken. The top priority, even more important than boiling the kettle for a brew or locating the bottle opener and corkscrew, is to get all your gear tidied away, because until this is done you won't be able to get everybody on board.

In case you think I am exaggerating, let me briefly describe the start of our first trip. Surveying the mountain of bags, suitcases, boxes of supplies and all the baby's clobber piled on the wharf, I despaired of ever fitting it all inside. As Selina, Jillie and baby Guy disappeared into the cabin, Max and I began passing our luggage onto *Woodstock*'s rear deck. Soon the girls were pleading "Don't bring anything else till we've found somewhere to put all this stuff!" As baby Guy began crying, Bill puffed on his pipe and strolled up and down the wharf commenting enthusiastically "Trim little craft."

Ten minutes later, as the baby's wails reached a crescendo, the heap on the stern was no smaller. By now Bill was muttering "Time we got going. What are they doing in there?" Jillie and Selina, alternating between cramming our provisions into the very limited storage space and trying to pacify Guy, took some time to clear a path through the boat. Once the rest of us were allowed on board, Jillie and I realised why we had so many boxes of groceries. As well as ordering some supplies through the boatyard, both of us had taken the precaution of bringing most of the items on our agreed list plus a few extras, so we had three duplicate boxes. As a result there was enough baked beans, ketchup and cornflakes for a regiment and a year's supply of washing up liquid.

Most first-time boaters bring too many of the wrong sort of clothes. For daytime you need things which you don't mind getting stained or splattered with creosote, oil, grease, or paint (usually black or white). Working canal locks is a very 'hands-on' activity. It is also a 'backside-on' one. In the evenings you are just a tad unlikely to need your dinner jacket or tiara; you'll probably be overdressed in a tie. Don't think smart restaurant or nightclub, but rather the *Queen Vic* or *Rover's Return* on a quiet night.

Storage space for your clothes and personal belongings may be rather limited, but bringing only one set of clothes and wearing them all week may not prove a solution that will endear you to your companions. Indeed living at close quarters, as you all will be for the duration of the holiday, the personal hygiene and habits of each crewmember will have a significant impact on everyone else's enjoyment of the experience. It may not be easy to find out in advance what disgusting or merely annoying practices your fellow boaters will bring on board. You may be embarrassed to ask people "Do you clip your toenails at the breakfast table?" or "How many times do you visit the toilet during the night?" but I believe you should know before inviting them. You can be sure of learning this and a lot more about your boating buddies before your week together is over – always assuming you manage to remain 'shipmates' that long.

It is also important to know if your companions snore. Unfortunately, people who do rarely admit it and most culprits are genuinely unaware that they nightly shake the rafters. On one trip a lady in our group bellowed every night like a somnolent hippo, yet each morning she appeared bright as a button, the only one of us who could say they'd had a good night's sleep.

Any children will by now be arguing over the top bunks, discovering how to climb up into them and how to fall off them. Older members of your crew are more probably inventing reasons why they must have a bottom bunk. Teenagers will be testing out the on-board stereo system with the volume button on 'full' and everybody will be nervously taking turns to inspect the diminutive toilet compartment, each hoping they won't be the first person who needs to use it.

Within thirty seconds of crowding into your canal boat's cabin everybody will be only too well aware why they are called 'narrow'. Individuals with any tendency to wave their arms about when talking will soon get sore knuckles and elbows, while boaters of ample proportions will literally have to squeeze through some sections of

Individuals with any tendency to wave their arms about when talking will soon get sore knuckles and elbows.

the boat. Trying to pass any of your colleagues could lead to moments of unappreciated intimacy! Because of this shortage of space, the dining table converts at night to a double berth. Unless you booked a boat with a fixed double bed and your better half stakes your claim to it immediately, the dinette could be where you'll be sleeping (I use the term loosely) as all the bunks will have been grabbed by everyone else while you were sorting out the chaos on the wharf.

Canal boats' foldaway bunks and dinettes can be quite ingenious, but remember to wipe the gravy and ketchup off the table before you put the cushions on it to make your bed each evening. Until you get the knack, converting the dinner table into your bed could prove too great a challenge for a tired and/or alcohol-affected brain to master, so you may spend the night on the floor. At least you won't fall out of your bunk if you do.

If, deciding there was safety in numbers, you've brought a fair sized party, at your first meal you will find out what the brochure really meant by 'large dining table'. Provided all of you are pencil slim, everybody may be able to sit around it together, just. Within minutes of squeezing them all into the area called the saloon (sorry the 'spacious modern saloon') you notice for the first time how surprisingly large some of your fellow boaters are. By the end of the week you will all have developed 'The Mealtime Sway'. In this traditional boating ritual you take it in turns to lean forward while those on either side lean back. After grabbing a mouthful of food you can then lean back and chew while your neighbours take their turn to scoop up a mouthful of their meal.

What with the strangeness of your surroundings and the narrowness of the bunks, nobody will sleep well on the first night unless they drink so much they're unable to stir from their bunk the next day. Some of your party may not sleep much all week, not only because of the restlessness of their cabin mates, but due to the variety of strange sounds in the night, such as the agonized yell of someone stubbing their toe on their way to the loo, what sounds like gravel being poured onto a tin tray just above your head whenever it rains or a muffled voice from the next cabin whispering "Shhhsh. Keep quiet or they'll hear us!"

Other factors which can (and probably will) keep you and you crew awake include the grating of *Blissful Daze*'s hull against the concrete bank, water slopping against the hull inches from your ear and overhanging branches scratching against the cabin sides. Then there's the nearby railway whose trains have a masterly knack of thundering past every time you manage to doze off.

The chances are that however badly you sleep the first night, you will wake up (as in no longer be able to lie in you bunk) quite early the next morning. There are several reasons for this, disregarding your excitement and enthusiasm to start the day. Perhaps someone sleeping on one of the upper bunks will fall out. This is quite difficult to do quietly, at least for adults. Our children could do so without hurting themselves, (amazingly once even without waking up) but grown-ups seem to make more of a fuss. Then you will find the dawn chorus (the real thing not Dawn Cruisers' fifty footer) creates a din louder than any alarm clock when the feathered choristers are only feet away. In case anybody is still dozing, the local duck population will call between five and six am to inspect *Blissful Daze*'s hull. This they do by noisily nibbling all the way along the waterline to check for tasty morsels of weed. Finally, to help the waking process, daylight will brighten your cabin. You may find that your boat has especially thin curtains that let the sunlight flood into your cabin each morning.

If nature somehow fails to totally rouse you and your canalling cronies, the job will be completed by some fellow members of the human race, although you may have a rather different description for a herd of anglers, wheeling their squeaky trolleys and talking loudly, as they head off along the towpath around dawn for a day's amusement dangling their lines. You could also find it hard to love your neighbour, the owner of the nearby boat, *Peace*, when he starts up his thudding on-board generator at six a.m.

Still, you haven't paid all that money to lie in bed all day. Now, as you struggle into some clothes and get the kettle on the gas, you may begin to realise, if you haven't done so already, that Ratty was right about there being absolutely nothing like messing about in boats. Look outside quietly and you might even see him.

4 *Which way?*

"Given a guide to the waterway,
you can always find yourself on the map."
[**Inland Cruising** by Tom Willis.]

BEFORE you were let loose with *Blissful Daze*, Gary will have come on board to show you how everything works. As he rambled on about various switches and knobs and the daily engine checks, you may have found it hard to take in if you were worrying about essential items that you'd left behind, like your reading glasses, waterproofs or wallet!

When Gary asks if you have any previous boating experience, he doesn't mean using the ferry or an hour on your local boating lake. By the time he has finished his 'talk-through', if your mind has gone blank, make sure, if nothing else, that someone has a note of the telephone number of the boatyard, so you can ring them on your mobile phone if you have any problems; you did remember your mobile, didn't you?

If you or your shipmates have set their hearts on visiting an interesting town or city, make sure *Blissful Daze* is pointing in the right direction. Here's a useful tip for the novice hirer: ***If your boat is pointing the wrong way, get your boatyard instructor to turn her round before he abandons you.*** It may be necessary to produce a steaming mug of tea (well sugared) and a slice of home made cake to ensure his co-operation, but it will be worth it. My second tip is: ***Always bring your mobile phone and a large cake with you.***

If you chose a boatyard close to a lock, Gary will probably show you how to work through it. The trouble is he will make it look very easy, just wait till you try doing one on your own! Gary will either have other hirers to instruct or want to get home, so don't expect him to stay with you for long. He will probably hang around to check if one of you can steer *Blissful Daze* a hundred yards without hitting both banks or other craft and then, once he has finished his tea and cake, he'll leap off at the first bridge, give you a cheery wave and wish you a good trip. From now on it will be your responsibility if *Blissful Daze* rams any other boats and before long you will have to puzzle out how to operate those locks on your own. If you aren't feeling too confident here's another useful tip: ***Pull into the bank near the first lock you meet on the pretext of searching for something you've dropped overboard.*** Then just wait for some other boaters to work through the lock. This way you'll all have the chance to watch them demonstrate how it ought to be done, or not, as the case may be.

Many hirers are determined to tackle 'a ring'. Blissful Boats may have suggested some to you. Unlike on 'out-and-back' trips, *ringers* won't see the same place twice, which for crews that have upset the locals could be a very good thing. But the advantage of retracing your steps is that you can go more slowly, get a second chance to explore all those pubs and villages you missed in the first half of your trip, and also to revisit those you particularly enjoyed the first time, or which you can't remember too clearly.

From most boatyards there will be a choice of routes, some with more locks than others. Faced with twenty-one locks, one after the other, or several hours cruising along a lock-free pound, the decision may be an easy one unless you and your crew are uncommonly keen to tackle locks. You may not need to decide straight away, but sooner or later THE BIG DECISION will have to be taken. This is usually, by tradition, done at the pub. Tip Number Four: ***Always know the whereabouts of the nearest pub.***

I suppose the simplest way of planning your cruise is to have no plan at all. I once shared a lock with a boatload of laughing canallers who told me they always started off in whichever direction their hire boat was pointing when they took it over, and turned round half way through their week. Another time I found a group who were so laid back they not only had no map or canal guide with them, they didn't even know what canal they were on or where they were travelling towards.

The potential problem with this approach is that such a crew may fail to get their boat back to their hire base at the end of the week; always assuming they ever leave it! At the opposite end of the scale are crews who plan every minute of the day: 'Start up at 8 am, then sixteen miles in the morning. Lunch in the *Dog and Duck*, through the fourteen locks by tea and moor up outside the *Jolly Fisherman* at 6.45 on the dot.' That's more like work than a holiday, but a lot of us have done it!

One aim on our trip on *Woodstock* was to experience the Pontcysyllte Aqueduct, which we did almost as soon as Bill had steered her out of the boatyard. There weren't any signs to warn us, but this is only wide enough for boat traffic to travel in one direction at a time. When we arrived there was an approaching boat halfway across, so we had to wait. But by the time the oncoming crew had reached us another boat had started across. After the fourth boat of a seemingly endless stream came into view, we persuaded Max to walk across the aqueduct and hold up the next boat so we could take a turn. Patience is a very necessary virtue on the canals sometimes! At this spot you also need a head for heights.

As *Woodstock* glided over that unpronounceable aqueduct, Bill puffed on his pipe and glowed with satisfaction, and decided we would push on down the canal as far as we could that evening. Each morning our skipper rose early and started up the engine while most of us were still in bed, so we covered quite a few miles during our week and had most of our meals 'under way'. Because he was much senior to the rest of us and had both naval and canal experience, we fell in with his routine, but it was Bill's possession of an artificial leg and a winning smile which ensured that he always got his way.

You won't have been on board very long before you learn more about the wicked tricks of the sliding roof hatch. Although trapping unwary fingers is good for starters, this demon's main prank is to wait until you've got used to the rear steps and then, the next time you're merrily climbing them to the rear deck, "CRUNCH!!" Your skull collides with the hatch and you collapse in an ungainly heap, blocking the gangway while everything spins before your eyes. One of the really handy things about boats though is that you are never more than a few feet from a bed. As you rub away the pain and call for Brandy, you can reflect on the fact that all experienced boaters wear caps. On deck this is to protect them from bird droppings and similar hazards, but perhaps they began the habit to soften the blow from their boat's sliding hatch. So my final and most important tip for novices is: ***Pack a sturdy cap and a stiff drink in your luggage.***

One writer suggests there is nothing worse than finding no corkscrew on board. I can think of several; how about a blocked toilet? Or a flat battery? Or mildewed bedding? However, taking your own corkscrew is a good precaution. Part of the unique fun of your first canal holiday is making a list of all the things you will take with you next time – assuming you'll be mad enough to go again! Checking the inventory that Blissful Boats sent you (if they did) you could easily fail to spot that something vital won't be found on board. On that first trip of ours we only discovered at Sunday breakfast that there were no egg cups. Everyone was grabbing for the tea towel at the same time while chanting something like a tribal war chant "Oooooh ahhh Ooooh!" as we tried to grip our steaming eggs and stop them rolling off the table. Wrapping them in tissues didn't work because by the time there were enough layers to keep hold of the eggs without burning our fingers, they were invisible amid the mass of paper which only served to cushion the blows from our spoons. These were the usual lightweight type which bent if you put too much sugar in your tea. After this debacle we cut the egg carton into segments and used these for the rest of the trip. Boaters, as you could well discover, have to be resourceful.

Keen canallers often plan their route in advance with a cruising guide. During the weeks before your holiday you can have hours of amusement puzzling over the strange symbols, trying to get to grips with 'lock/miles' and studying the diagrams explaining how to operate locks. Even more useful, you can check out where all the shops, pubs and off-licences are.

Once you begin your cruise, however, it will become clear that your canal guide leaves out a lot of the important details that you really need to know. Never mind; you will get plenty of entertainment writing in your own amendments and additional notes, such as 'Very shallow!!', 'Limited moorings'. Awful beer', 'Excellent beer', 'Fish & chips', 'Water tap out of use', 'Collided with camping boats', 'Towpath impassable' or 'Lost crew'.

On *Woodstock* we were given a cruising log for writing down interesting details of our voyage. These can provide a fascinating record of your experience. My log for that first canal holiday has an intriguing entry for Monday "1815; Pipe hunt commenced: unsuccessful." This requires explaining. Bill hadn't been able to enjoy his usual puff as he'd steered the boat during the afternoon, because he'd mislaid his pipe, and a thorough rummage through his cabin failed to locate it. So, once we'd tied up, everyone, except the baby, was pressed into making a fingertip search of the entire boat. Still we drew a blank. The mystery of the missing pipe occupied us all evening and remained unsolved the following morning. It was only around coffee time, while I was steering, that Bill's voice called out triumphantly from below "I've found it." The lost pipe had been discovered inside his false leg. It must have slipped in there after he unfastened it when taking his regular after-lunch nap. On all future holidays with him, we insisted that Bill pack a spare pipe.

5 *There must be a name for it!*

"Canal travel can seem a complicated affair – especially for beginners."
[***Canal Mania*** by Anthony Burton.]

WHILST there are 'correct' names for every part of canals and the boats to be found on them, as well as the various evolutions inland cruising requires, unlike our salt water cousins, it is not considered essential to know or use most of them. For instance, while to an Old Salt like Bill they were lines, hawsers, warps, painters, halyards, stays, sheets or shrouds, (sailors seem allergic to using the word 'rope'), on a narrowboat you can safely use this word for everything thicker than string. You may also be relieved to know that sheets belong on a bed and no one would dream of mentioning shrouds.

Bill had a tendency now and then to lapse into seadog-speak, calling out to other steerers 'Mind your helm!' or "Watch your starn!' One splendid trick he employed was The Sailor's Deaf Ear. If another steerer tried to tell him anything he didn't want to hear, Bill would give them a fixed grin, cup his hand to his ear and yell 'Can't hear you over the engine, Skipper.' Before turning in every night he always went on deck to look at the sky and 'check the warps', but Bill knew that on the canals the use of too nautical language is actually frowned on as being pretentious. When he talked about port he meant the tasty red liquid in a bottle.

All activities seem to develop their own peculiar language, often inventing brand new words which flummox the uninitiated. With canal cruising it isn't so much new words but the new meanings given to old ones that can confuse the newcomer from the moment they step aboard. Here is a guide to the main culprits.

BANK: You will need to go to yours to withdraw plenty of cash before leaving home because they are very scarce along the canals. The sort you will find runs along both sides of the canal to hold the water in place. If any of it is missing your holiday will come to an abrupt end.

BEAM: This could refer to the width of your boat, or your hips, or your smile if you win the Lottery. However on the canals it is short for 'balance beam'. This is that chunky length of wood or metal used to swing lock gates open or shut. They make useful seats, but got their name because they are meant to balance the gate; occasionally you may find one that actually does.

BOATER: A type of flat straw hat popular amongst sporting young men in the Victorian age, but now a term for people who are 'boating'. So this is a polite word for describing you and all the members of your crew for the next week. Sometimes it may be qualified by a less-than-polite adjective.

BOW: Some of your more notable achievements you may feel entitle you to take one, but Murphy's Law says there is only ever an appreciative audience for your mistakes. The front end of the boat has a number of names that grows every time it crashes into someone else's property, but we will stick to calling it the bow.

CUT: This is the familiar term for the canal itself, rather than ignoring someone on purpose, sneaking off school or a small accident with a knife which results in half the boat being smeared red and using up the entire contents of the first aid box in one go.

DRAUGHT: There may well be one (or more) on *Blissful Daze*, particularly if there's a north easterly wind blowing, but this is boat-speak for how much of your boat's hull is hidden below the surface of the canal. Only on dry land does it refer to a pint of Best Bitter.

FLIGHT: If your boating holiday starts in the pouring rain you may wish you had booked one to somewhere warmer. On the canals it means a group of locks close together and some exercise for your crew.

LIST: You'll probably have to make these for shopping most days if your crew are very hungry, but this is also the word for what your boat gets when everybody stands on one side of her. If it becomes bad enough someone may fall off and reduce *Blissful Daze*'s list whilst increasing the list of casualties.

MOOR: Not a reference to a famous Shakespearean character (even on the Stratford Canal), but the act of tying up your boat, i.e. *parking* it, but please *NEVER* let anybody hear you use that word on the waterways.

PADDLE: This doesn't refer to the seaside activity, but a sliding underwater trap-door at each lock that lets water in and out. To 'draw a paddle' means to open it, not get out your pencil and sketchpad.

Someone may fall off and reduce Blissful Daze's list whilst increasing the list of casualties.

STUD: Whatever you may think, this is the name for the bit of metal at the front end of the boat to which the mooring rope ought to be secured.

WAKE: Most mornings you may do this earlier than you intended, but it's only when *Blissful Daze*'s propeller is thrashing the water that you'll see her wake. If you're the steerer don't stare at it too long or the bow will collide with something.

WASH: On small boats you may have to do this in the galley sink (preferably not when it is still full of last night's dishes), but this word also refers to the waves your craft ought not to make by going too fast. It is considered bad because it damages the banks, soaks anglers' feet and upsets their tackle and tempers.

WIND: (Rhyming with 'tinned') Apart from that natural element which can make boating particularly tricky when it blows too hard, and quickly passing over that embarrassing bodily condition all too often encountered below decks, 'to wind' is the proper expression for turning your boat round (intentionally) with the help of the wind. A 'winding hole' is the usual place for attempting this entertaining manoeuvre.

Other terms you'll be using like an old hand by the end of the week include Locks, Gates, Tiller, Boathook and Towpath. Locks are the box-like chambers that boats use to go up or down hill. They are very popular (and tiring) on some canals. To 'lock up' doesn't mean gaoling members of the crew, even though this may at times seem like an excellent idea.

It may take a day or more to stop calling lock gates 'doors'. As you will learn, these unco-operative devices have several little tricks to delay you and to make your boat's passage more challenging for her crew and more amusing for everyone watching.

If your boat doesn't have a steering wheel – and most canal craft don't - her tiller is the stick on the back deck which you will spend many hours pushing left and right to keep her pointed in the right direction.

A boathook is a very dangerous piece of equipment that can be used to prod lock chamber walls, collect samples of mud from the bank and make holes in fibreglass boats that get too close. Lash your boathook upright to the side of your boat and you can fly the Jolly Roger from it.

As towpaths provide access to the canal for non-boaters such as motor cyclists, dog walkers and fishermen, you might think you would be better off without them, but then you'd have no way of getting to the locks or village shops and nowhere to tie up. Unless you volunteer to steer, you could spend a lot of your holiday tramping along the towpaths; be warned.

At your first lock your crew should have a chance to use those right-angled metal objects which everyone has been tripping over since you boarded *Blissful Daze.* Some people call them 'lock handles', others 'lock keys', but to most canallers they are a 'windlass'. However, new crews (and some not-so-new ones too) may be heard calling out "I haven't got my whatsit." and "Where's the winding thingummy?"

Watching other people working boats through locks has fascinated people for so long that the old boatmen coined a name for those who do it: 'Gongoozlers'. So now you'll know what to call any idlers who laugh at your first attempts at boating – add your own adjectives and/or expletives as appropriate.

As craft from the same hire fleet have identical colour schemes, always check you're on the right one. Returning from a shopping expedition or an evening at *The Jolly Boatman,* it can be embarrassing for you and disturbing for the occupants of *Blissful Maid* which you mistakenly board instead of your own. How would you like it if a gaggle of strangers tried to break in just when you were in the middle of doing something you don't need an audience for?

One final point: it will be useful if your crew know their left from their right. For those who have problems, some ingenious solutions have been invented, as I learned on a visit years ago to the old Museum of Science and Technology in Birmingham. A portly, balding member of the staff with a generous smile told me the story of the narrow boat captain whose wife got them muddled up. Each day he used to put a piece of bread on one side of the cabin roof and a lump of cheese on the other. Then, when he wanted to give her instructions on which way to steer he would call to his wife 'Push the tiller towards the cheese' or 'Bring her over to the bread.' A likely tale!

6 *Practice makes perfect.*

"Do not consider you have any competence
until you have spent several days afloat."
[**The Shell Book of Inland Waterways** by Hugh McKnight.]

THERE's nothing quite like it, that thrill of steering along a canal for the first time, although your confidence may be dented slightly when one of your crew asks "Are you meant to drive on the right or the left?" or "Won't it damage the boat scraping along the concrete like that?"

Most canal hire boats have tiller steering, which is excellent because the boat responds immediately you swing it left or right, but not so good until you realise that *Blissful Daze* will turn in the opposite direction to the way you expect. Once this has been mastered, you will find that one of the greatest joys of cruising is watching someone else having their first bash at steering a long canal boat; and I do mean 'bash'.

Nearly all young children let loose on the stern of a narrow boat have this incurable urge to waggle the tiller left and right, left and right, merrily thumping the handle into all the adults within range. But older novice steerers are just as bad and do the same thing when their boat is moving, as though tiller waggling is what drives their craft forward rather than a turning propeller. Those in the minority – the non-wagglers – try desperately hard not to move the tiller at all, even when this is rather urgently needed to change direction. No, they grit their teeth, grip the tiller tighter and hold the same position, presumably *willing* their boat to turn.

Neither approach will work on *Blissful Daze*, and she will continue to bump, thump, crash and bash into things until her helmsmen and women get the idea of making small adjustments in the right direction. It may take an hour or two, and for some of your crew rather longer, but everyone gets the hang of it sooner or later; well, almost everyone.

It can be wonderfully relaxing cruising along with the canal to yourself. But then you'll meet a bridge. Bridges, like ponies, can spot a novice a mile away and enjoy giving them a hard time. Most canals have lots of them and their tendency to suddenly move sideways the moment you have *Blissful Daze* lined up may be a tad un-nerving. When tackling bridges there are four useful rules to remember:

1.) You stand a much better chance of getting *Blissful Daze* through the navigation arch if she approaches bridges straight rather than sideways on.

2.) Although some bridge holes are wide enough to pass oncoming boats, others very definitely are not.

3.) All bridge arches are very solid. Despite fragments of brick or concrete falling on your boat, in any encounter you must expect the bridge to come out on top, literally. Just look at the scratch marks along some boats' roofs and the paint left by them on the masonry of most low bridges.

4.) Don't panic! Steel boats are remarkably tough – even if they do bend a bit. Yours is a steel one, isn't it?

As well as bridges, you will soon have to cope with an even worse waterway hazard: *people*!! Other people using your canal come in two sorts: those on the water and those on the land. ***Watch out for both***!

If the canal seemed narrow when you had it to yourself, the space will look even more restricted when you have to squeeze *Blissful Daze* past a boat coming towards you, and it will be a lot harder to avoid a collision if their bow weaves about as much as yours.

Bill's advice as I had my fist stab at steering *Woodstock* past an approaching boat was "Hold your line and let them steer round you." I did as he said, and the other skipper moved out of our path and promptly ran aground. All her crew gave me a withering glare as we glided past. The next time I pulled further over to the right, and *Woodstock* ran aground.

Perhaps you'll do better, or maybe the trees will get you. If the overhanging branches of one, or more, of the millions of trees which stick out along the water's edge don't manage to smack you in the face, they'll whip your mug of tea or glass of wine off the boat's roof before you can mutter 'Blissful Boats!' Don't say you haven't been warned.

With so much beautiful nature and fascinating things to look at, it is easy to lose concentration. This is not wise if there are anglers ahead. Most fishermen (and occasionally the female of the species) may be spotted in the distance as a large clump of equipment littering the towpath. Apparently the modern angler needs this mass of rods, nets and containers, as well as their seat and a gigantic umbrella, to follow their hobby. A few wear camouflage clothing and then cunningly hide behind enormous clumps of reeds or giant bushes so that passing steerers fail to spot them until their boat is within inches of the protruding rod. If you don't slow down they could react in a not altogether friendly manner.

Boaters and anglers have to share the canals and most wish the others didn't exist. So take the moral high ground, slow down, keep a steady course, avoid their tackle and give them a cheery "Good Afternoon!" and they'll ignore you entirely.

As your boat will mow down their lines if they don't remove them, anglers don't have much choice but to let you and *Blissful Daze* pass. But many will wait till the last millisecond before shifting their rod, and then lift it upright so you and your crew have to risk their squirming maggots dropping down your necks. Still, they don't have much to laugh about.

What with bridges, boats, the local vegetation and anglers, you'll have plenty to contend with, not to mention your crew. Already you may be questioning the wisdom of bringing several individuals and making plans to *accidentally* lose them en route. When, in their usual tactful way, one of them draws your attention to the fact that *Blissful Daze*'s bow fender is bearing down on a tiny glass fibre dayboat by yelling at full blast ***"Watch out for the people in that little boat!"*** you may only avoid sinking them by bouncing off the steel piling or ramming the nearest tree. After taking as much abuse as you can stand, it is time to suggest that someone else hold the tiller: not just anyone, but the person who has been giving you most grief. Now is your chance to turn the tables on them. With a bit of luck they will soon meet a boat on a blind bend and panic! As soon as they biff *Blissful Daze*'s bow into a bridge, collide with another boat or ram the bank, you can get your own back with a suitably cutting quip, such as "I imagine you're pretty good on the dodgems!" or "I'd sue that optician of yours, if I was you." Following this little episode, things may settle down and you can all start to learn together.

It is probably better for any discord to be out in the open rather than to simmer for days and then suddenly erupt with the unhappy individual telling you "I've had enough. I'm going home, NOW!! I can't stand you ordering me about every minute of the day. Do this, do that, with never a please or thank you. Who do you think you are anyway, Captain bloody Bligh?" This may all have begun with a seemingly innocent suggestion to a weighty individual that they move to the opposite side of the boat to reduce her list. So watch out.

As a novice on the canals, you are going to make the odd mistake, but if you are surrounded by a load of incompetents they may not notice when, despite applying full throttle and creating a seething wake, *Blissful Daze* doesn't move away from a mooring because you forgot to untie the ropes. If you keep quiet, it may be several days before they realise that ramming the bank prior to mooring is not the standard method.

Even the most dim-witted hirers should realise that their boat is pointed at one end and sort of round at the other. They will probably also be able to tell you before the week is over that the boat always goes 'pointy end first'. Unfortunately, this isn't quite true because, on occasions, (far too many for most novice crews) *Blissful Daze* will need to REVERSE!! Canal boats are not good at this. Inexperienced steerers tend not to be good at it either! The problem isn't that their propellers can't run in the opposite direction to forward, but that narrow boats don't steer too well going backwards. In fact, many boaters will tell you that in reverse **they don't steer at all!.** So, when it's your turn to reverse *Blissful Daze* back down the canal, I hope you don't have to travel too far. You will discover this technique very definitely falls into the 'hit-and-miss' school of boat-handling. And whether you hit or miss all the other boats around is in the hands of the Gods, so say your prayers and take it slow.

If you have young children on board you may think you're a genius when you retrieve an empty milk bottle crate from the canal and then little Sam or Samantha standing on it finds they can see over the roof well enough to steer. They'll really enjoy this, but don't trust them to make sharp manoeuvres, or else they'll fall off their pedestal and land in a heap of tears, while *Blissful Daze* ploughs into a heap of trouble.

Unluckily boats don't have brakes. A hire craft attempting an emergency stop can be heard several miles away. As her throttle lever is rammed full into reverse, her engine will give a complaining roar whilst belching vast clouds of blue-black exhaust fumes. The boat's progress will slow a little as she then slews drunkenly across the canal. When you try this, *Blissful Daze* may finish up aground and smothered by dense bushes on the other side of the canal, or she may succeed in jamming each end into opposite banks so as to completely block the navigation.

Max and I took it in turns to stand on the bow as lookouts and to shout a warning if we spotted any boats coming the other way. When Bill couldn't hear what we were yelling, we invented a system of hand signals. Unfortunately my skipper tended to be more confused than helped by our unconventional semaphore and had to rely on Selina translating. I can't help wondering how a holidaying 'tic-tac' man would signal sighting a traditional pair of working boats approaching around a blind bend. Probably the same as the rest of us, by rushing back through the length of the boat yelling "STOP!! STOP!! **STOP!!!**"

7 *All tied up.*

"Nothing could be simpler than banging in the stakes."
[Tony Soper quoted in Hire Boat Brochure.]

IF you think controlling *Blissful Daze*'s movements when under way is all you have to learn, you are in for a jolt, just as she may be any time you are moored. For, surprising as it may seem, you probably won't be the worst steerer on the cut and some other airhead may disturb *Blissful Daze* and all her crew by ramming into you whilst you are relaxing.

Scattered around the canals there are thousands of bollards and rings, mostly sited where you are forbidden to moor to them, such as those at water points, immediately above and below locks and those prime mooring spots reserved for 'permit holders only'. However, thirsty boaters (is there any other sort?) are welcome to secure their craft to those outside pubs; and they do. Unless you stop early, you may have problems ever discovering a space large enough to get *Blissful Daze* into. Apart from other hire boats that get there first, you could develop a suspicion that some private boats, like *Ale & Arty, Boozer's Delight* and *Meinzapint* spend all their time on these moorings.

As well as the opportunities for the steerer crashing *Blissful Daze* into any boats moored nearby, tying up offers plenty of scope for the rest of the crew to provide brilliant free entertainment for any lounging gongoozlers. Because boats don't have brakes, bringing *Blissful Daze* to a halt in a gap only a few feet longer than her hull is something of a test of nerves as well as skill. She may head into the bank alright, but when you tell her to stop, she will just keep on drifting forward aiming her bow fender for the rear end of the next boat. Crunching into the stern of the craft moored ahead of you is one way to do it, but this technique is unlikely to bring out the best in your neighbours, particularly if they were just in the middle of serving up a meal or enjoying a drink!

If you can put some of your crew on shore and get them to hold onto her ropes, *Blissful Daze* can drag them along the towpath until they slow her down. But if your shore party refuses to indulge in a bit of 'towpath skiing' and won't pull on the ropes, the skipper may quickly become both worried and hoarse. Ideally your crew will haul on both bow and stern ropes at the same time and heave *Blissful Daze* close to the bank. However, if there is an underwater obstruction, when the bow rope team put their backs into it, the bow may swing towards the bank, but *Blissful Daze*'s rear end will move the same distance away from it. After a barrage of yelling by the back rope squad to advise their counterparts that they have overdone things, the stern will be pulled back to where it was. Unfortunately, at the same time the bow will now swing out again. This seesawing can go on endlessly until the skipper either calls a halt or everyone collapses from exhaustion.

If all the stronger (i.e. heavier) members of your crew heave at one end while the featherweights hold the rope at the other, the first group will sprawl in an untidy heap on their backsides as the others fly head first off the bank and take an unscheduled dip. This should delight any lurking gongoozlers as well as making an excellent photograph.

Your attempts to moor could be equally humiliating if some over-keen plonker leaps off at the bow with a line and ties it too short. Then the fun really will begin. Now, not only will the helmsman find it impossible to bring the rest of *Blissful Daze* into the bank, her stern will try to swing away from it. Once her steerer gives up ineffectually revving the engine, they may grab the nearest rope intending to hurl it to the crew on shore. As it flies off its cleat and lands in the water they frantically grab a boat hook only to find the rope has drifted out of reach. *Blissful Daze* continues to swing until she lies right across the canal and everyone on the rear deck has to fight off a mass of spikey bushes overhanging the offside bank. A lengthening queue of boats builds up, increasing both your audience and your embarrassment. Eventually, it occurs to someone to slacken off that front rope, and, once your other line is retrieved, the stern can at last be secured. Following this little fiasco, you may remember that even mooring rings and bollards have to be used with caution.

All bollards are not identical. Some have been designed so that however carefully you wind your ropes round them, they will quickly leap off again. This can lead to all sorts of embarrassing situations, such as when you attempt to use *Blissful Daze*'s stern rope to bring her to a stop ahead of a lock but she runs on and rams into the gates with a jarring thud. Or, even worse, as the skipper tries to moor alongside the packed beer garden of the *The Barge and Blunderbuss*. If, after leaping ashore and stylishly taking a couple of turns round the post, the devilish rope suddenly slips off, leaving you to topple backwards finishing up in a large rose bush, your pride and not a little else may be rather dented.

Alongside canals there are a lot of other potentially good things to put your ropes round, such as telegraph poles, trees, railings and road signs. Unfortunately, using any of them generally leaves your rope obstructing the towpath, which is a cardinal sin. My friend

John has a favourite story about one time he had an encounter with a gang of waterways maintenance staff. Edging his boat, *Lillian Rose*, past their moored work-boat, where the crew were having a tea break, he decided to tie up while preparing the nearby lock. John was just about to put his rope around a convenient sapling in the hedge, when, as quick as lightning (which is very unusual for a waterways employee) one of the men called out with some feeling "Oi, you can't tie your rope across the towpath, **even we're not allowed to do that!"**

When you eventually do moor up (in reality often decided by the hunger or thirst of the crew rather than the skipper) if there's nothing to tie *Blissful Daze*'s ropes to, you may be able to use piling hooks if there are any on board. These bits of bent metal can be very useful, but watch out! They have several tricks they can play, such as refusing to fit on the piling you want to tie to, unhooking themselves if your crew jiggles about too much or when a boat passes in the night, and refusing to let go of the pilings when it's time to leave your mooring.

Otherwise it's time to fish out those mooring pins (also known as pegs, stakes, spikes or 'those ******* ******s') and to search for the boat's mallet. It is now that you will find out what a necessary bit of gear this is, and also that they have an unfortunate tendency to go missing. I reckon the chances of a novice crew getting through an entire week without losing their mallet is about equal with those of a narrow boat sailing round the world. You may wonder why, therefore, Blissful Boats don't provide a spare one. Of course the answer is very simple, they know most hirers would lose this as well.

You will now discover that the piece of towpath selected for banging your mooring pins into is either like concrete or suet pudding. Often it is as hard as concrete for the very good reason that it is concrete, with a thin layer of grass on top, just to dupe you; but compacted canal mud has an almost identical consistency. Getting your stakes into ground like this can produce a lot of cursing, ringing in the ears and numbed fingers, together with a feeling of exhaustion that can only be cured by the consumption of quite a lot of alcohol.

Don't be fooled into thinking that soft ground is any better. True your stakes may disappear underground at the first bash from the mallet, but wait until a boat goes by driven by some maniac who thinks he's practising for powerboat speed trials on Coniston Water. Then your pins will either lean over until the ropes slip off, or else fly out of the bank to land with a plop in the middle of the speeding boat's wake. In either case you will be adrift and called upon to take urgent action. It's no fun wading through nettles in your pyjamas in the dark.

As with most items boaty, the mallet has an alternative name, 'the lump hammer', presumably because whenever you whack your thumb with it or drop it on your foot a colourful lump soon appears. Another trick they have is for the head to fly off. If this happens and it doesn't make a dent in someone's skull, it will either disappear into the canal or a bramble thicket. Now who is going to try to retrieve it?

Whether using your boat's pins or something more permanent, tying up depends to some extent on using knots. As any nautical language is likely to increase our bafflement, it won't help if some know-all babbles on about hitches, falls and bights. To most of us this rapidly becomes a haze of technical mumbo jumbo. Bill couldn't teach me, and as for learning from a book, when I tried I got lost on page three – and that was a Ladybird title!

Blissful Daze's lines may be in good condition or fraying, knotted travesties, but you can be sure they won't be the right length. If they are very long, you and your crew will spend all week struggling with armfuls of wet rope and falling over their snake-like coils. If, however, they're on the short side, everything you want to tie to will always be tantalisingly just out of reach, and every time your crew try hauling from the bank, they'll end up slithering into the canal.

Any members of your crew more likely to throw themselves into the canal might best be excused.

It is probably a good idea for everyone to learn how to throw the boat's ropes; although any members of your crew more likely to throw themselves into the canal might best be excused. Watch other crews to see how to do this, and how not to do it too. In response to a shout from the canal bank to "Sling us your rope." there's a good chance of seeing a boater toss an armful of rope neatly into the gap of water between his or her boat and the canal edge. By the time they've recovered the rope for a second attempt, the distance will have doubled and the rope will now be sodden. You could open a book on their chances of missing with their second throw. If you must add a photo of this performance to your growing collection, please try not to embarrass your victim too much; it may be your turn soon.

Whenever Bill saw what Max or I had done with a rope, he flinched. He was obviously appalled at our un-seamanlike knottings, but he never said anything unless our ropemanship was so substandard that *Woodstock* was in danger of taking a journey on her own. And you do need to watch out for this tendency in hire craft. Most of the time Bill just chewed the stem of his pipe, whistled under his breath and made sure we were the ones who undid the knots when it was time to 'cast off', as he always called it.

I can't tell you what knot I use, but somewhere along the line I seemed to acquire it, and it works, I think. My family are quick to remind me of the various occasions when boats which I tied up have drifted away from the bank, but I always put this down to outside interference, as I still do. My advice, for what it's worth, is to find a knot (or something vaguely resembling one) which you like. Never mind if the Worshipful Company of Knot-tiers would not recognise your efforts, remember the old slogan "If it works, use it." Mind you, there is one important proviso to this rule, it helps if your knot can be untied in under ten minutes.

When novice crews are attempting to tie up or to leave a mooring the result is often a complete shambles, and a very noisy one at that. The complaining whine of the over-revved engine is usually nothing beside the complaining from the skipper that his crew are all incompetents and not following his orders, and from the crew that the skipper doesn't know what he's doing. Soon everyone is yelling at everyone else and the scene becomes even more confused as more experienced boaters offer their advice. It has to be said that there could be a fair amount of shouting during the first few days of your trip.

After everyone on board *Blissful Daze* has turned in for the night, a stranger will wander along the towpath and, for reasons I can't begin to guess at, do his utmost to trip over your mooring ropes. There is little you can do to prevent this, although some boaters tie bits of white rag or shopping bags to their pins. Try to be philosophical; if the towpath trekker doesn't catch his foot on your rope he will almost certainly find something else to fall over, so don't worry, just make sure your stakes are in firmly enough so that his clumsiness doesn't wrench them out of the ground.

In the morning, struggling to extract their pins from the towpath can leave boaters feeling weak until opening time. If you spot a boat steered by a man with a very red face, it might be due to over-indulgence the previous evening, but being charitable you may decide it is the result of heaving and straining to pull out his uncooperative stakes. Give him the benefit of the doubt, a smile and a wave.

I can't finish this chapter without a few final words about ropes. As you will quickly discover they can be awkward, self-knotting, embarrassing bastards!

8 *Look out for locks!*

"The carefree manner of cruising along a lock-free stretch of waterway comes to an end as soon as the first lock comes in sight."
[**Inland Cruising (A guide to boating on canals and rivers)** by Norman Alborough.]

As *Blissful Daze* arrives at your first lock your heart beats a little faster (for some boaters a LOT faster). Is it the thrill you feel at the prospect of tackling this new challenge that excites you? Or is it fear of making a complete bungle of the whole business and looking an absolute prat?

What did the hire company brochure say? "Locks are easy." Oh yes! Perhaps you've studied the page in your cruising guide and know exactly how to operate a lock, ***in theory***. Now is the moment to find out if you and your crew can put in into practice – take a deep breath and go for it.

Scenario A.

A narrow lock and there's nobody else about; no-one to watch, no-one to ask, nobody to give you a hand if you start sinking the boat! After several nervous minutes spent bringing *Blissful Daze* into the bank and tying her ropes to those handy white bollards, you all walk up to the lock and look at this rectangular challenge. Some Jeremiah then offers a helpful comment "We'll never get the boat in there, will we? It's not wide enough." Of course they can't be right, your boat must fit in there, just.

The cruising guide says to open the gate. Eventually someone has the common sense to realise that this may be achieved by pushing that big chunky piece of wood. So everyone lines up next to it and tries to move it. The gate won't budge. This is not surprising as half of you are trying to push the balance beam one way and the other half are pushing in the opposite direction!

It is the skipper's responsibility to sort this out and soon everyone is pushing in the right direction. After heaving and straining and a lot of grunting the gate still refuses to move. Ah! Hopefully you remember reading that the gate won't open until the water makes a level. And how will you know when it has made a level? When it does so, you'll be able to open the gate!

Someone then suggests "Shouldn't we let some water in or out?" Of course that's what those L shaped winding things are for. Where do they go? Weren't any of you paying attention when Gary explained it to you at the boatyard? Then somebody fits their windlass on a spindle and winds up a paddle and things start to happen. "Oh that looks easy enough!" thinks everyone else with a windlass, and before you know it paddles are being wound up all around the lock. NO! How long will it take to realise that if the paddles at both ends of the lock are up at the same time, the water will just flow through the chamber?

At last the water does make a level and the gate easily swings open. Now all you've got to do is steer *Blissful Daze* into the lock. For the first day or so, just persuading their boat's nose into a lock chamber, especially narrow ones, may be sufficient challenge for some steerers, but, by the time you're tackling your third or fourth lock, it may dawn on you that it might be better to throw the throttle into reverse BEFORE *Blissful Daze's* bow smacks into the gates at the far end.

After a few more locks you may find it is possible to slide her in without alternately biffing each side several times. Don't get over-confident and please do remember to check the gate is open before trying to steer *Blissful Daze* into (or out of) each lock.

Scenario B.

On arriving at your first lock there is another boat approaching it from the opposite direction. Don't be too quick to congratulate yourselves on your good fortune. They may be one of the Smouldering crews from Furnace Boating Co. This company paint their boats in a distinctive lurid red, yellow and black livery and specialise in hiring their sparsely equipped sixty footers to groups of lager-drinking students. Their craft can usually be heard at least four miles away courtesy of the ghetto blaster on the roof thundering out the latest hit sounds at one million decibels.

If, as you prepare to take *Blissful Daze* up her first lock, *Smouldering Inferno*'s crew appear, WATCH OUT!!! Before you have time to think, two strapping teenagers may compete to see who can raise their paddle fastest. As the slower of them takes all of two seconds, before you are aware of the problem, a tidal wave of water escaping from the lock will sweep down making poor *Blissful Daze* lurch backwards, twist sideways, and wobble about until she finally subsides with her stern now firmly wedged into the bank and her bow wallowing unchecked in mid-channel. As *Smouldering Inferno* exits the lock, you may be on the receiving end of what her crew think is hilarious wit, as you struggle to pole *Blissful Daze*'s front end out of their path. Try to remember to grab hold of the less muddy end of the shaft.

You won't fare much better if you've just got *Blissful Daze* into the lock when *Smouldering Volcano*'s crew descends on you. Before you can stop them, they'll slam the bottom gates shut behind you and whip up both top paddles. The sudden surge of water will make *Blissful Daze* buck and lunge as much as any pony about to be branded and your crew will need to hang onto her ropes like cowboys roping a wild stallion. If you can't hold her, she'll rebound off the bottom gates before surging forward to crash into the other end with a mighty reverberating shudder.

If you are ever short of a topic of conversation, try canvassing your crew's opinion on whether they would rather be on deck or inside the cabin when *Blissful Daze* experiences one of these violent collisions. The steerer, only too anxious to avoid everyone's accusing stares, may prefer the relative safety of the cabin, but the galley slave, doubled up by her impact with the fridge, then pelted with flying plates, saucepans and bottles before being thrown to the floor to writhe amongst heaps of spinning potatoes and cans of soup, will pick the deck every time. Any member of the crew idling in the front cockpit – who will probably have been instantly reduced to the state of a cowering jelly – may wisely suggest that the only safe place to be is ashore, or, better still, at home.

Dropping down locks provides even more opportunities for embarrassing gaffs. Make the mistake of not keeping the stern far enough from the top gate as the water level drops, and you may begin to sense that something is wrong when the front of *Blissful Daze* starts to tilt down and your crew cry out in alarm as they hurtle towards the bow. Or you could make that most classic of boating blunders and tie up in the lock. If your ropemanship is like mine, the knots may not hold, but if they do, the likely result is that as the water level drops the ropes will break, the posts you've tied to will tear out of the lockside, or the cleat will give way with a violent snapping sound. What I don't believe can really happen is for your boat to hang suspended in mid air, as suggested by the cartoonists. This is surely impossible, isn't it?

Taking *Blissful Daze* through wide locks will provide you with slightly different challenges. You may find yourselves *sharing with another boat*! On *Woodstock* we met our first wide lock at Bunbury, which is a staircase, so we had the double delight of trying to fathom out how to operate them while dropping down the flight with a private boat called *Heaven's Door*. Her skipper was smartly turned out in a green tweed suit and bow tie while his mate, as I remember, wore her hair in a bun and sat down a lot. Once we cleared the bottom lock, they tied up. Whether it was the trauma of sharing the locks with *Woodstock* or because they needed to use the boatyard's facilities, I don't know, but we were left to continue on our own with Bill telling me "Chester by sundown, my boy. Chester by sundown."

Because we had a reasonably smooth ride going down the series of locks leading to Chester, we weren't prepared for their tricks when we returned back up them the next morning. Bill still refused to bother with ropes, and so poor *Woodstock* occasionally threw herself across the lock chamber, biffing into the wall with a mighty 'clunk'. After one specially violent side-swipe, Jillie appeared in the bow cockpit with a pained expression on her face, which only worsened when *Woodstock*'s stern bashed into the wall with another reverberating thud. Somehow, though, Guy slept through it all – the little star!

On the canals, as wasting water is considered a sin, boaters are encouraged to share locks whenever possible. So when we caught up with a middle-aged gentleman gently working his wooden cruiser, *Woodpecker*, up towards Christleton, we asked if we could share the next lock. But he had seen the un-roped *Woodstock* lurching about in the previous lock, and, after very firmly declining our suggestion, he tied *Woodpecker* to the nearest bollards and hid in his cabin.

You can hire boats from the boatyard at Bunbury, so novice hirers beginning their holiday from there are faced with a steep learning curve and an opportunity to test their brain cells as much as their muscles. When we reached these locks on our way back there was already one boat in the lower chamber and another waiting beyond the top gates but not daring to enter. Under Bill's direction, I took *Woodstock* into the bottom lock and he sent Selina to tell the second boat to enter the top chamber so we could ascend. Now it is quite simple for one boat to cross with two coming the other way in a wide staircase, but some tentative skippers take a lot of persuading of this. Conversely, there are a few less cautious ones who don't realise that two boats won't be able to cross with another couple coming the other way. It would be highly entertaining though, to watch the results of four narrow boat crews attempting this!

One of the first lessons lock-workers need to learn is which is the right side of a balance beam to stand. Loitering in the wrong place can lead to pain, a sudden ducking and instant notoriety. And it isn't only boat crews who are at risk on lock sides. Even innocent spectators can make the mistake of gongoozling from the wrong spot. After peering down to watch a boat enter the chamber, they may fail to hear someone yell "Watch out!", and only realise who was being shouted at when the solid bulk of a massive balance beam strikes them in the small of the back and catapults them into the murky depths.

Most locks have ladders so that people can climb out; which only goes to show what a common event this must be. There are several different ways to fall into a lock and you may discover them during your cruise. But toppling you into the water is only one of the variety of tricks that locks like to play on unwary canallers.

You won't have travelled through many locks before you appreciate how fiendishly cunning, as well as varied, canal locks can be. It's amazing how often that curved line of raised bricks, instead of providing a foothold, only tries to trip you up, and how the tread you really need at the very edge of the lock is usually missing, while the one at the other end of the quadrant has been positioned so that only people seven feet tall can use it to push the gate open.

And then there are 'blowholes'. As you whip up a ground paddle there's a whoosh of air and a jet of cold water shoots out of the ground by your ankle and straight up your leg – very invigorating! At narrow locks you will probably see other boaters casually stepping across the bottom gates when one of them is open. This saves time, but do you dare try it?

Whether or not you become confident moving around the locks, by the end of your holiday some of you should at least have learned that no amount of pushing and straining will make a gate open before the water has made a level. If you meet a school outing there will probably be ten children struggling to open each gate while the chamber is still half full, but this is probably encouraged by the teachers as a way of tiring the kids out. Don't copy them, your crew will need all their strength for winding the paddles, mooring up and getting down to the pub this evening.

Returning to using paddle gear – for you will have to again and again – it's surprising how little hire company brochures include on the difficulties their customers may experience in winding up some of them. If you meet a particularly stiff one you might think that a weight-lifter would make a useful addition to your crew, but on second thoughts you'd never squeeze him into a narrow boat, let alone seat him round the dinette table.

Although the only way to learn how to operate locks is to do it and keep on doing it until you get it right, before leaving the safety of your own home you could try reading up on the subject. Better still, get hold of a copy of an instructional video. BW produced one some years ago to show how canal cruising ought to be done. This came complete with an aggravating soundtrack on which a cluster of musicians constantly fiddled away drowning out much of the narration. I reckon BW got their marketing strategy all wrong with this creation. Although quite informative, it made desperately dull viewing. They could have had a best seller on their hands if instead they had compiled a video of ***what really happens at locks***.

9. *A few complications.*

"If a crisis occurs and you are heading out of control for another boat, four knots seems more like forty at the point of impact."
[**Kiwi Afloat** by Doris Coppell.]

THE gentle chug-chug-chug of the engine and the rippling of the water against the bow as, with growing confidence, you steer *Blissful Daze* along the tranquil canal, drinking in the scenery and the sunshine and, with luck, the occasional glass of alcohol. Ah yes, that's what you came for - 'sheer magic'.

Make the most of it, because before long something is sure to crop up to interrupt your carefree reverie, like a junction for instance. Unfortunately for steerers wishing to change canal, many waterway's junctions were very inconsiderately designed; particularly for the novice. Not only may the canal you are trying to turn *Blissful Daze*'s bow into have the narrowest entrance possible, but, just to complicate things, there will frequently be a large bridge blocking the view. This will make it impossible for you to see any boats that are coming the other way, or for their crews to spot you. At junctions collisions between boats are quite common!

Bill handed me the tiller as soon as we got off the Llangollen Canal. I was just starting to relax when there was the entrance to the Middlewich Branch, which we planned to explore. The next few minutes still haunt me. I over-revved the engine, totally misjudged the turn and *Woodstock*'s bow crunched into the brickwork several feet wide of the entrance. My only comfort was noticing the large number of scars on the masonry left by previous incompetent navigators as they'd biffed and bashed their way around this corner before me.

Junctions are an excellent place to give a few blasts on the boat's horn. Some hire boats have a nice raucous one that carries well. This is far better than those which produce a pathetic 'peeep' thatsounds like an asthmatic sheep. The only drawback with a really loud horn is if crewmembers lounging in the bow cockpit have a heart attack every time you give a good fruity blast. Remember to listen out for other boats' sound signals and be prepared to stop *Blissful Daze* in her tracks. One advantage of steering, as opposed to resting at the front of the boat, is that you're much further away from the point of impact when head-on collisions occur.

In your week *Blissful Daze* may not need to turn round, but then again she might. This could be because you forgot to turn off at a junction, reached the end of a canal cul-de-sac, or decided to head back to base because your crewmembers are exhausted after working so many locks. Turning a boat is called 'winding' and, as it would be rather a nuisance for other boaters if craft attempting to turn round were constantly getting wedged across the channel, on most canals there are a few wider places known as 'winding holes'. These are often very easy to miss, so if you are making an out-and-back cruise you'll need to take care that B*lissful Daze* doesn't live down to her name and coast straight past the spot where you need to turn her round. The next place where you can wind could be many miles and hours away. Crews making this mistake have found themselves cruising supperless late into the night desperately searching for the next winding hole by torchlight.

Selina and Bill had already made it look quite easy by the time I made my first attempt to wind as *Woodstock* prepared to leave Chester. When we cast off, Max shoved her bows away from the bank while I pushed the throttle forward and swung the tiller across, however, instead of turning into the winding hole, *Woodstock* obviously wanted to go on down to the Northgate locks. I was sure we were going to smash sideways into Cow Lane bridge. As he watched my efforts, Bill sucked on his pipe and smiled encouragement. I put on full reverse and Max took hold of the boat pole and began stabbing the water with it. Little by little the bow began to swing into the winding hole, so I tried more power and our bow fender rammed into the brickwork. Jillie, Selina and Guy all complained loudly! With *Woodstock* creating masses of foaming wake, her stern crept slowly round and Max struggled to fend off a section of concrete wall. At last, when I thought I'd successfully completed the turn, Max tried to push the bow to the right by thrusting the long shaft into the canal bed. Unfortunately he found a soft bottom and was soon yelling at me to slow down as the pole wouldn't come out of the mud. Max slithered along the gunnel towards Selina, Bill and I clutching the top of the pole and we just managed to heave it out of the mud's clinging grasp before being swept off the stern deck.

Winding holes are amongst the spots where anglers are not supposed to set up camp, so there may well be one dangling his line from the bank when you want to use it. You can try apologising, but I don't know what good it will do, or you could tell him he isn't supposed to fish at that spot, which will probably result in total silence or a lengthy moan. Most boaters use the same ploy as the fishermen and just pretend the other isn't there. There's also a fair chance that you'll find some stupid boater moored up in a winding hole! You and *Blissful Daze* won't commit that crime, will you?

Winding your boat is certainly a manoeuvre that provides the perfect opportunity to make a perfect idiot of yourself. If the winding hole has been properly dredged and no other boats appear, you may get round quite easily, but to be quite honest, I'd bet against it. If you succeed in wedging *Blissful Daze* across the canal or finish up stuck fast in the middle of the winding hole, don't worry, before long some helpful crew will arrive and help pull you clear. It's called the 'camaraderie of the cut' and they won't object if you offer to buy them a pint at the next pub.

By the end of our week afloat we weren't too bad and only made quite small dents in the canal bank when winding *Woodstock*. On our final morning at Llangollen everyone watched with surprise as I successfully winded the boat while Jillie did the same for baby Guy.

On our approach to Chester we'd met another complication, Th*umper*, a boat that had come adrift and was blocking our way. Faced with this situation you may be tempted to charge her at full speed. Please don't. A less vicious tactic would be to nudge *Blissful Daze*'s bow against the obstruction and try to nose it out of your path. This may not produce the result you are hoping for, as *Blissful Daze* will probably start to skew sideways and finish up alongside the drifting boat. So now there will be two of you blocking the canal.

This situation, we decided, calls for the Captain to order "Boarders Away!" and for a couple of your crew to scramble across to the floating road-block and pole it out of the way. Then, if you are very conscientious, you'll take the time to tie the drifter to the bank. If, on the other hand, you aren't quite such Good Samaritans, once *Blissful Daze* has squeezed past, you'll leave her drifting about in mid- canal so the next crew along can try out their own technique for tackling this sort of waterway hazard.

Meandering along with the sun on your back and the sound of birds twittering all around, it is remarkably easy to forget about steering, until you're suddenly snapped out of your daydream by an hysterical yell from the bow. This is when you find out if you've got the tiller business sorted. If, without time to think, you instinctively move it the correct way and avoid colliding with the bank, bridge, tree etc. you've made the grade. Well done. If, on the other hand, *Blissful Daze* now rams the bank, scrapes the bridge or collides with the tree, put on the dunce's hat.

If you're enjoying a quiet doze in *Blissful Daze*'s front cockpit while someone else takes the responsibility of zig-zagging her down the canal, you could experience the crews on passing boats, instead of giving you a cheery wave, pointing at the front of your boat. When you don't react they shout as they glide by "...something under the bow." This may prompt you to lean out and take a peek to discover that a length of planking, a large branch or a section of fencing is caught there.

This offers a chance to use your boathook. Should you sidle along the side deck to collect it from the stern or leap onto the roof? Either way, try not to get knocked off by passing bridges, trees etc., etc. Armed with the boathook you can try releasing the trapped debris from under the bow. It is unlikely you will be able to pull or push it free until *Blissful Daze* slows right down, but it is another entertaining activity unique to canal cruising. Oh yes, and don't lean out too far...

It has to be admitted that sometimes on canal holidays the weather is not quite perfect. There may be the odd gusts of wind or period of torrential rain to add to the challenge of your boat-handling. The wind can be (and is) used by helmsmen as their excuse for just about everything. It's much more believable though if there's a fair amount of it blowing around at the time that you grind *Blissful Daze* against the concrete, scrape her along a line of bushes, wallow sideways into a patch of reeds, bash her into the lock approach wall or thump her into *Merry Ways*. The wind rarely helps on the canals (except for drying your wet clothes), but it frequently makes keeping control of your boat more of a lottery.

Another natural phenomenon you will be lucky to avoid is rain.

Sometimes on canal holidays the weather is not quite perfect.

This will affect *Blissful Daze* in a number of ways. If it rattled on the cabin roof all night you may be even more bleary-eyed than usual in the morning, and some crews don't seem quite so enthusiastic to come out of a nice warm and dry cabin to help with mooring up or working the locks in the middle of a downpour. Hopefully it won't take too long for your crewmembers to realise that it's better if they don't go inside in their wet weather gear, dripping over everyone's bedding and soaking the carpet!

If your whole crew are drenched in an unexpected cloudburst there could be a bit of chaos and nudity below decks as everyone (except for the poor steerer who has to stick to their post) struggles to change into dry clothes. Then there will be a bit more chaos as everyone (except you-know-who) tries to find somewhere to hang up their dripping clothes to dry. By the time the helmsman is relieved there will be nowhere for their sodden clothes to dangle and drip. Let's hope the sun comes out again soon!

One final complication we met with at the end of our first week was a trip boat being towed by a horse. Apart from the decoration they leave on the towpath, horses aren't much of a problem, but their towropes certainly can be. Get on the wrong side of a horse-drawn boat, and, as well as receiving some choice comments from her crew, everything on *Blissful Daze*'s roof will be comprehensively swept overboard.

There are a few other minor matters that may complicate your cruise, but overcoming unexpected difficulties is all part of the enjoyment of boating holidays, and I wouldn't want to spoil your fun by preparing you for every eventuality. Besides, *Blissful Daze*'s engine may not break down and you may not get her jammed in a lock. With luck you won't run out of money, diesel, water or food, lose your boat's mallet, 'watermate' key or all the windlasses, nor find yourself faced with a mutiny or sink.

10 *Falling in with other crews.*

"As you learn how to master the locks friendly boaters are always on hand to share a laugh....."
[**Hire Company Brochure.**]

On a canal holiday you will meet lots of other boaters, whether you want to or not. Expect to develop better relations with crews on boats travelling in the same direction as *Blissful Daze*, not only as there will be more time to chew the fat, but also because some of your encounters with approaching boats will begin with a collision, or, at least, a close shave.

As Dogberry comments in *Much Ado About Nothing*, "Comparisons are odorous." but it is very hard not to judge your own skill, or lack of it, against other crews you meet. This tendency will prove particularly strong if you find *Blissful Daze* cruising in company with her sisters: *Blissful Beauty* and *Blissful Summer*. How you will glow if their crews are even worse duffers than yours and you see them make a complete dog's breakfast of approaching a lock or mooring.

If someone from another boat says "It looks like you've done this before." your ego will receive a terrific boost, but don't let it go to your head; it won't be long before your inexpertness catches you out and brings you back to earth with a bump. As well as being shouted at, greenhorn boaters can also expect their blunders to provide passing canallers with quite a few giggles.

On our trip on *Woodstock* we enjoyed hearing about other hirers' experiences and comparing their boats with ours. Locks and moorings provided good opportunities for chatting to friendly crews and sneaking a look inside their cabins, and so did those all-too-frequent queues at water points.

If you should meet a boat from Brown's Budget Boat Co., be sure to check her out. After seeing her galley, your cooks should be a lot less picky. You will probably have already judged the standard of this fleet from their tattered fenders and frayed ropes and the absence of paint on the hulls of *Brown Booby* and *Brown Creeper.*

If there's one company that can give Mr Brown's outfit a run for their money it's Carefree Canal Hire Co. You can get an excellent idea of their boats from *Jolly Roger*. You'll probably spot her moored up somewhere, as the Carefree fleet spend a lot of time not moving. Expect to see her with her stern sticking out at an awkward angle and her bow rope fixed to a tree. Her stern line – all ten knotted feet of it – will most likely be tied to the sheet piling.

While pretending not to do so, you can all steal a surreptitious glance inside *Jolly Roger* as *Blissful Daze* chugs past. A brief glimpse is enough to confirm that a week on one of this company's boats would be anything but 'carefree'. This experience should make your crew much more content with your choice of vessel. *Blissful Daze* is the height of luxury compared to *Jolly Roger*, which makes even *Brown Booby* look good!

By contrast, you'll be hard put not to stare open-mouthed at some of the more luxurious hire boats around, such as *Splendid Sylph* and *Splendid Surprise.* Splendid Cruisers seem to attract kid glove hirers who insist on using the boat's ropes at every opportunity.

This is very commendable, but it can be just a tad aggravating, when your crew are hoping to be inside *The Narrowboat and Newt* by lunchtime, to find you are working up a flight of locks behind *Splendid Salamander,* whose six crewmembers insist on ever so carefully pulling her into and out of every lock. It may take all your self-control not to bawl out at them "Why on earth don't you use the ******* engine?"

There are plenty of mid-range hire companies, such as The Easy Boating Company and City Hireboat Co. So, if you get the chance, peek a look inside *Easy Edwina* or *Birmingham Betty*. The ideal opportunity to check out other boats comes when they've broken down or stopped to sort out a problem. If they accept your offer to help search for their missing weed hatch cover, or release their ropes from the grip of the steel piling, you'll have the chance for a friendly chat and a sly nose around at the same time. With luck they may even ply you with coffee and chocolate biscuits.

Every day you will be bumping into other crews and how you control *Blissful Daze* will affect how they react to you. As you cruise along a delightful stretch of rural canal bordered by bushes and trees, spare a thought for the owner of *Costafortune,* a private seventy footer with a smart new paint job, who considerately tries to make room for *Blissful Daze*'s zigzagging bow. As a protruding branch is heard gouging a continuous groove along the full length of her cabin side, don't be too surprised if the passing crew give you something less than friendly looks or gestures.

Most people you meet though will respond with a smile and a wave. Some may offer advice, such as reducing your speed, learning to steer or taking a little water with it, but generally other boaters will prove to be good humoured. Most of the time, but not always.

My very first conversation with someone on another boat took place at the pretty Shropshire town of Ellesmere. Bill steered *Woodstock* down the short canal arm on Sunday morning as we were in search of that most elusive of creatures; a milkman. Bill neatly stopped with the bow fender one foot from *My Dream*, an ageing green boat moored across the end of the basin. A middle-aged woman with tousled brown hair, pallid complexion and a worried expression appeared from beneath its canopy. “I thought you were going to hit us.” she confided, “That would have been the last straw.” I didn’t know what to say, but obviously, now she had begun to unburden herself, this pathetic figure meant to make the most of the opportunity. “We’ve been on this boat a week and it’s rained every single day and the roof leaks like a sieve...” As she continued to regale me with a catalogue of woes, I was mightily relieved when Bill reversed away. We had such a game turning *Woodstock* round for the first time that we forgot all about the milk.

If sometime, as you gently nudge the tiller this way and that and wonder when your next snack is going to appear, you vaguely notice a line of boats beside the towpath with people idly standing beside them turning in your direction, it may be a good idea to stop. If you go pottering past, you could find yourself and the crew of *Blissful Daze* on the end of a few ripe comments about queue barging, or be accused of not having the sense you were born with. For, chances are, this is a queue for the locks and you will have to take your turn. Once *Blissful Daze* has tagged on at the back, even if that means an embarrassing test of your boat reversing skills, you will be treated much more kindly and soon be chatting away to the crew in front about important matters of the day such as the weather and the nearby pubs.

Approaching crews may smile and wave, or only give you a grudging nod of recognition, but occasionally they’ll call out a warning about some peril ahead. Note what they tell you and keep a sharp lookout. Perhaps there’s a broken-down boat blocking the channel, a dredging gang at work, golf balls flying overhead or half a mile of anglers in a competition. Other possibilities include the local farmer trying to rescue one of his heifers from the water, kids playing on a home-made raft or maybe a boat that is about to appear through the bridge just ahead of *Blissful Daze*, in which case you’d better SLOW DOWN!!

In the midst of all you amateurs messing about in boats for the fun of it, there's just a chance of you running into a pair of genuine working boats. There are three very different types on the canals: cargo-carrying, camping and hotel boats. In the case of real working boats keep well out of their way at all costs – their crews take no prisoners! The crew on camping boats, such as *Rough* and *Ready* or *Mishap* and *Mischief,* won't be in such a hurry. They can usually be spotted at a distance as each craft is festooned with dozens of excitable children wearing brilliant orange buoyancy vests. They all leap off at the locks and hurtle about like demented ants while their leaders try to teach them the basics of 'working through'. Conditions on board some of these boats are even more basic than on *Smouldering Cauldron* and *Brown Noddy*, and very different from hotel pairs like *Gourmand* and *Gourmet*.

The guests on hotel boats don't have to lift a finger if they don't want to, but they may leave their gin and tonics long enough to saunter ashore with their cameras to snap the professional crew working the locks, and lean against the occasional balance beam. Met on a flight of narrow locks *Gourmand* and *Gourmet* may hold you up. If this happens use the time to cadge a drink if you can. One writer even claims to have got a free cooked breakfast this way.

Apart from the crews on boats like *Smouldering Volcano* and *Brown Booby*, most of the boaters with whom you'll 'graze gunnels' will be like yourselves, a ragbag of individuals or two, three or even four generation family groups, relying on their own skills and ingenuity. So you should find a ready rapport when you catch up a crew struggling to keep their boat under control or to get her moving, and can offer your help, for what it's worth. Watching them straining to raise a reluctant paddle will at least warn you of its stiffness, so you can make sure none of your geriatric crewmembers nor the children have to face it. No, you'll tackle it yourself, won't you?

During your trip you will probably encounter a sprinkling of Salty Dogs and Captain Bird's Eyes. I expect you know the types. The former wear battered peaked caps, chunky blue Guernseys, shapeless trousers and boots, are usually bearded and move with quiet efficiency as they puff on their old pipe. The latter stand out by sporting new boating hats covered with scrambled egg, are clean-shaven, sport a crease in their slacks and always talk very loudly while doing nothing practical at all. Salty Dogs don't often seem to have female companions, but as they like to see their craft operated deftly, their crews are usually small and efficient. By contrast Captain Bird's Eye is always accompanied by his 'good lady wife', typically dressed in a head scarf, brilliant floral top, woollen trousers and court shoes. She doesn't do anything either, which is why there are a number of extra personnel in such a crew, usually their children and assorted spouses, who have come along more out of duty than any interest in cruising.

People-watching is a very definite part of the boating scene, so don't forget that you and your crew will be providing entertainment for other people. Let's hope they are more amused than appalled by what you all get up to. On my canalling debut Bill steered us down the Llangollen so swiftly that we didn't get much chance to chat to other crews until we reached Beeston. Here we caught up with *Princess Lily*, her mainly female crew were vainly trying to coax her away from the bank and into a lock, but she obstinately refused to budge. Max, gallant as ever, offered to help push them off the mud. After a couple of minutes of their revving the engine and Max shouldering her cabin side, *Princess Lily* lurched and slithered off the mud and away from the bank. Unfortunately, Max now found his head and shoulders beyond the point of no return and plunged full-length into the two foot depth of liquid mud between *Princess Lily* and the bank. Moments later a spluttering bedraggled figure rose from the water crying out "Where are my glasses? Where are my glasses?" before diving back in again in search of his specs. After a frantic minute of splashing in the shallows, Max re-surfaced triumphantly clutching his glasses and received a second ripple of applause.

11 Round the prop.

"I was once stuck by Wigan Pier (yes, honest) with
a vast knitting of tights, bits of wire, a pullover, nylon netting,
a mat-like substance and dozens of plastic drinking cups
all bound together by oily goo."
[Magazine article by John Gagg.]

THE people who sell them claim that propellers are beautifully engineered works of art, which will thrust your boat through the water with the minimum of effort. In the case of canal boats this is a vile perversion of the truth. Their props are devilish devices that think their sole purpose is to attract as much rubbish to their blades as they can in the shortest possible time. They are so effective that *Blissful Daze* will probably have something wrapped around her propeller before the end of your first day.

If you're unlucky she may manage to do so by the time you leave the boatyard. The stuff they find hiding in the shallows of our canals, as well as being very varied, is also frequently loathsome. Anticipate having to remove something unpleasant from your prop every day.

Woodstock hadn't gone many miles before she misbehaved, slowing to a snail's pace, and a limping snail at that!. Bill tried increasing the revs. This produced plenty of noise, vibration and exhaust fumes, but little change in our speed. Then the tiller started to dance about as if possessed by a poltergeist and she became impossible to steer. Selina and I were ordered to leap ashore with ropes and Max acquainted himself with the procedure for disentangling the prop.

It probably won't be long before you spot a stationary fibreglass cruiser with her skipper dangling headfirst over her stern struggling to clear things off his propeller. Owners of this type of boat get plenty of practice inspecting their props but need very long arms to clear the rubbish wrapped around them. Most don't mind too much discovering a load of weed or even barbed wire, they're just relieved to find their propeller is still attached!

By contrast, most boats with inboard engines provide an ingenious obstacle course for you to overcome to get at the propeller, except for traditional narrow boats, whose props can only be cleared by hanging over the stern with a boat hook or standing waist deep in the canal. As hire companies rightly assume most of their customers wouldn't be too enthusiastic to do this, their boats are all designed with weed hatches.

To make the task of clearing things from the prop a bit more entertaining, these hatches are cunningly placed in the most inaccessible spot beneath the rear deck. Each is covered by a vicious metal lid held down by bolts that usually don't like being undone; but, before battling with these, you have to reach the wretched thing.

Your first step is to lift the deck boards. There seem to be two designs for these: awkward and ****** awkward! With one arrangement, after removing half the decking, you have to prostrate yourself on the remainder and reach down with one telescopic arm to undo the retaining nuts. Needless to say, these are sometimes rusty and may take a lot more persuasion than a gentle one-handed twist to release them. It is surprising how many uses you will find

The tiller started to dance about as if possessed by a poltergeist.

for *Blissful Daze*'s mallet during your trip. This is just one job it can help you with.

In the second design, after setting the deck boards to one side, you need to squeeze into the limited space next to the engine. When this procedure was demonstrated at the boatyard (if it was) the engine was cold. Now it is almost red hot and sizzling better than any barbecue.

About this stage *Smouldering Ember* or one of her sisters may come steaming past. If her wash causes *Blissful Daze* to rock, expect this movement to unbalance your deck boards, which will then land on your head. Always remember the importance of keeping young children well away from the stern while doing anything near the engine, not so much for their safety, but to prevent them hearing the string of expletives spat out by adults at times like these. Now move the deck boards further away and try again. Whilst struggling to loosen those reluctant nuts you will probably scorch your backside on the engine block or burn your arm on the exhaust, or both, resulting in more expletives and a search for the First Aid box.

As you lift off the weed hatch cover, try not to remove the skin from your knuckles and don't drop the beastly thing overboard. Now is the moment to be brave. Plunge your arm up to the elbow into the square hole and feel around the prop for whatever delightful rubbish is responsible for this interruption to your cruising. There is an old chestnut of a story that a hirer, having opened his weed hatch, solemnly began trying to bale out the water before clearing the prop. Can that be true?

To stop customers losing their weed hatch covers, some companies, like Pretty Narrowboats, have hinged ones. With this ingenious design, when the unwary hirer tries to investigate whether it is twenty feet of barbed wire or only fifteen feet of electric cable wrapped around his prop, the cover clangs down on his arm or shoulder. The procedure of clearing the prop can't then be continued until his wounds have been treated, a barrage of insults hurled at the offending chunk of metal and somebody finds a suitable wedge to hold the criminal open. All boats in the Pretty Narrowboats fleet come with a pretty large First Aid kit.

It does sometimes happen that what comes up through the hatch actually is weed, but there's a fair chance that you will find something much more revolting. Rotting plastic sheeting, manky cushions, tyre inner tubes, rolls of oily carpet and bags of putrefying meat are just some of the interesting items I have retrieved through the weed hatch. Don't worry though, you probably won't manage to find quite as much in only a week.

Something newcomers do all-too-frequently discover coiling itself around their prop is their own boat's rope. Many novice boaters only realise what they have done when they look for this line to pull the stern into the bank so they can investigate the mysterious obstruction to their propeller. Then the awful truth hits them, and for the rest of their holiday they have to make do with a shortened stern rope with a huge and ugly knot in it.

When you reach down through the open weed hatch, taking care to avoid the cooking engine, and rest your chin in a convenient patch of grease, an angular piece of metal will prod you somewhere painful. After working out how to minimise these distractions, you will learn that clearing the prop requires both the flexibility of a contortionist plus using a selection of tools – such as wire cutters and a hacksaw – which hire boats never seem to include in their inventories.

In an average week's cruising you can expect to collect, and have to stop to remove, any (or even all) of the following treasures from your prop: fishing line, shopping bags, fertiliser sacks, binder twine, seemingly endless strands of wire – both plain and barbed – plastic tape, odd sized bits of tree, miscellaneous items of clothing and lengths of rope. Mind you, picking up rope (other than your own) is not always bad news, particularly if you manage to stop the engine before it's chewed to shreds, as you may gain a handy length to supplement your boat's rather scrimpy supply. If *Blissful Daze* succeeds in chopping up her mooring lines you could be glad of any extra lengths you manage to retrieve as you go along.

On his initiation Max only found a plastic bag, some binder twine and a few thousand decomposing leaves. Like many a hirer both before and since, Max cut the prop free with the aid of the bread knife and kitchen scissors. If you find that these tools on *Blissful Daze* are a bit on the blunt side, the chances are they've been employed quite a few times before to hack through a variety of materials caught on her prop. I hope you washed both well before using them in the galley.

A few miles further on and it was my turn to undergo the ritual of the weed hatch initiation. My first problem was moving my audience far enough away so I could stack the deck boards at a safe distance. Max kindly called out "You'll find the retaining clamp is a bit stiff, here, hit it with this." and went to hand me the mallet, but as I was trying to avoid scorching my legs on the exhaust, I didn't quite grip the handle in time and it clattered into the bilges. Once I'd removed the hatch cover, I apprehensively delved into that gaping rectangular hole. At least the water was clean. I soon found a tight parcel of brambles and binder twine clinging to the prop shaft and Selina brought me the scissors from the galley. Unfortunately I'd only succeeded in cutting through one strand when they slipped out of my hand never to be seen again. By the time I'd unravelled several yards of twine, *Woodstock*'s bow fender was investigating the bushes on the off side and her stern had swung close to the bank. A private boat called *Dunworkin'* had caught us up and her crew kindly asked if we were okay. Bill, puffing on his pipe, waved them past and they nervously edged alongside and then gradually pushed our boat out of their path. As her steerer came level with me he grinned and said "That's one less for us to worry about." How I wish I could have come up with a suitably witty and cutting riposte, but I couldn't think of anything to say. As I screwed the weed hatch cover back in place, I secretly hoped we'd see *Dunworkin'* further down the canal with something really nasty round her prop.

It may just happen that your propeller will attract something that doesn't just make it churn the water more slowly, but actually stops the prop dead. If you do, the engine will cut out at this point, but *Blissful Daze* will continue to glide forward at a good speed for the next few minutes unless you can stop her with the ropes. If she is heading directly for *Rustling Wind*, a 'plastic' cabin cruiser, this may be the time to panic. Well, you should never panic, but the occupants of *Rustling Wind* might want to, unless they can move her out of your path.

Sometimes Lady Luck may smile on you and, instead of *Blissful Daze*, the boat ahead of her will catch the lurking monster. Then, as you motor carefully past *Happy Wanderer*, some unfortunate man (somehow females always manage to avoid this job) will be struggling to heave something simple, such as a lorry's tarpaulin, through her weed hatch. "Everything alright?" you call out helpfully. His reply will vary according to his temperament from "No problem, just a little rubbish on the prop; soon have it cleared." to a non-stop and completely unprintable tirade of abuse encompassing the waterways staff, the local population, the twenty-first century and mankind in general, all of whom don't know who their parents were and should never have been born in any case. As you move out of earshot, you may have to admit that your crew aren't such a bad bunch to spend a week with after all.

Let's close this chapter with the sorry tale of Algernon Copthorne-Browne, whose stylish launch, *Serendipity*, was sunk by leaves. It was a sunny autumn day and all was right with the world for Algy and his pals, until *Serendipity*'s propeller sucked in so many of the russet-coloured leaves carpeting the surface of the canal that she lost power. "Leave it to me chaps." volunteered Algy, "If you would just hold the ropes, I'll have the jolly old prop cleared in two ticks." With that he nobly stripped off his blazer, rolled up the sleeves of his Jermyn Street shirt and set to work. Five minutes later, as Ronald and Petronella intimated that standing on the bank holding a darned rope was not their idea of a spiffing day out, Algy, anxious not to delay them a moment longer than he could avoid, called out "All fixed." and replaced the deck boards, rolled down his shirtsleeves, buttoned his cuffs and replaced his blazer. Shortly after restarting their journey, the boat's handling become increasingly sluggish, but they only began to suspect all was not well when Aurelia was heard to exclaim "Gosh, that's dashed funny; I do believe my feet are wet!" Everyone, with the exception of Algy, immediately remarked that not only was there water on *Serendipity*'s carpet, but that it was growing deeper with every passing moment. Poor Algy's last exclamation before abandoning the helm was "Oh, bother! I believe I must have forgotten to fasten down the glug, glug....."

12 In the dark.

"Before you enter a tunnel, put young children in the cabin and have others under supervision – it is disturbing to come out of a tunnel with fewer children than when you went in."
[**Introducing Inland Waterways** by Charles Hadfield.]

LOOKING ahead, the canal appears to be blocked by a large hill, then, as the boat rounds a bend, the dreadful truth dawns. That tiny black semi-circle is where the canal disappears underground. Someone has got to take *Blissful Daze* through a tunnel and that someone is you!

Ideally, to get the full effect, canal tunnels should be so long that you can't see the far end when you chug into them, take at least half an hour to navigate – preferably longer - and inspire fear and trepidation into some of your crew. Harecastle does, and has an added treat for boaters heading north. Soon after the last boat passes through the southern portal a pair of iron doors clang shut behind it, the temperature drops, and a great whirring hum almost drowns out the throb of your boat's engine. Then, as a swirling mist fuzzes the view ahead, you will probably think for a moment that you've been entombed in a ghostly grotto and will never see the light of day again. Don't worry, the tunnel keepers will get the sack if fewer boaters come out of the tunnel than enter it.

When your crew realise you intend taking them all into that murky hole, one or two may express less than total ecstasy and turn very pale, or they may let fly a broadside of colourful language to let you know they wish to take no part in your subterranean activities. If anyone suggests "Why don't we just go round it?" resist the temptation to have them flogged at the gratings for stupidity.

Some landlubbers think tunnels are only suitable for miners and potholers. If you have any like this on board they may try to jump ship. Unless you are keen to lose them, foil their mutiny – locking them in the galley if necessary – because allowing members of your crew to try walking over the top of a tunnelis just asking for trouble. It is not unknown for crews trying to avoid 'the terrors of the deep' in this way to become so disorientated that they walk round in a circle and finish up at the same end of the tunnel where they started, or can't find the tunnel or canal at all!! If your shore party doesn't disappear never to be seen again, they may make themselves sick with worrying that *BlissfulDaze* has sunk in the tunnel or everybody on board had been suffocated by poisonous fumes. Besides, they would be silly to miss the delights of boating through these fascinating, dank, unlit channels lined with soot and decaying brickwork. True boaters think they are an essential part of the fun. So will your crew – maybe.

If there is a dreary, overcast day during your holiday, that would be the ideal one to tackle your long tunnel. However, that well-known law of Mr Murphy (aka Sod) will ensure that if you are restricted to only one sunny spell in your week, your tunnel will loom in front of *Blissful Daze* just as the sun breaks through the clouds. Whatever the weather may be like outside, it could be quite damp inside the tunnel. Some boaters get togged up in their full set of 'oilies' for every major tunnel, while other don't bother or rely on an umbrella for underground boating. I prefer my waterproof jacket and a glass of rum.

In wide tunnels your boat will be able to squeeze past those coming the other way – well, usually. But many tunnels are too narrow for boats to pass each other and at some of these boaters have to observe a timetable. This could cause a problem for crews who don't know what time it is or whether they are heading north, south, east or west. If you misread the timetable and meet an approaching boat when you are half way through, hard lines! The other skipper will have every right to insist on you reversing *Blissful Daze* all the way back out again. Now that would be both tricky and ignominious!

The Llangollen boasts three tunnels so we soon met our first and slipped through it without any major dramas, only nudging the wall slightly. However, the next, at Chirk, proved rather more challenging. Here our first problem was to get *Woodstock* into it. As we could see a distant headlight, Bill waited for the approaching boat to emerge. Just as it did so we spotted another headlamp gleaming in the blackness, By the time we'd seen half a dozen boats come out of the tunnel, Bill's patience was wearing rather thin. He suggested someone walk through the tunnel and stop the endless flow, but none of us was brave enough to volunteer.

Once *Woodstock* was in the tunnel, I was praying a short-sighted steerer wouldn't try to enter at the far end, Bill turned up the revs and Max tried making shadow pictures in the headlamp's beam. Mysteriously at this and every other tunnel passage we made, Jillie had to go below to check on baby Guy.

As soon as you steer into a tunnel don't be surprised if everyone previously clustered on the stern suddenly disappears. It can be a bit unnerving if you don't notice them leaving as the darkness deepens and, turning to make some comment about what an eerie feeling this is, you find you are talking to an empty deck. However, apart from your own incompetence and maintaining your regular supply of hot or cold drinks – because the galley slaves refuse to come on deck in the dark – the main problem will be other boats and their steerers.

It won't take you long to learn that steering inside a tunnel is different from outside. For some mysterious reason hire boats are afraid of them and, however hard you try to keep to the centre, most of the time yours will do everything it can to creep along the wall, bumping the brickwork every few feet. The only time boats don't try to hug the sides of a tunnel is when they are about to meet an oncoming vessel. Then they become seized by a sudden urge to veer into its path and cause a collision. So be on your guard and hold *Blissful Daze* in check. Unfortunately, there is nothing to say the approaching helmsman will be as diligent as you, and before the passing manoeuvre is completed there may occur a certain amount of grinding and scraping of hulls, for which you will be blamed – if not by the other steerer – then by the more fearful members of your own crew, whose apprehensions they assure you have now been fully justified.

One of the amusements inside tunnels is listening to the echoing of your voices as you yell or sing. There are crews that instantly burst into song the moment they enter one. This may in some cases be more a way of keeping up their spirits than celebrating their pleasure at cruising underground. Or it may be that they've already been at the spirits!

For any crewmembers who don't like tunnels, watching the TV isn't an option as there's no reception underground, but if there's a video on board, while you're on deck enjoying the spookiness of the tunnel, they can relax in the saloon with *Psycho* or *Nightmare on Elm Street*! According to warning notices you will pass, all gas appliances are supposed to be turned off while you are in the tunnel. I can't imagine that any crews stop cooking their roast dinner or making a brew in tunnels, and I'll bet that more than a few embarrassed canallers have slipped below for a crafty shower rather than let on that they were afraid of the dark.

The further *Blissful Daze* penetrates into the darkening borehole, the more you will become aware of the clunking, clattering and rumbling of her engine. Perhaps some people sing to drown out these noises. It will be reassuring for you if yours is a reliable engine. I hope for your sake it is, because tunnels are not good places to break down.

Part of the fun of tunnels, apart from their spookiness, comes from all those drips and waterspouts. If there has been a lot of rain the previous week these can be pretty hard for the steerer to avoid. It's a good idea to listen out for them, otherwise the first you know may be a sudden deluge of icy water down your neck. Most of the water falls from the roof, either as a narrow torrent the helmsman can try to dodge, or as a tunnel-wide curtain which there is no escaping. Occasionally there may be the additional treat of a horizontal spout catching you on the side of the face or filling your shoes. When *Blissful Daze* passes through a particularly generous example of these natural showers, the crewmember who hung their laundry to dry in the front cockpit may wonder why they bothered and start counting their remaining clean clothes in a desperate hope that these will see them through to the end of the trip.

Some boaters turn on all their interior lights in tunnels, but I think this is unsporting Besides, the darkness is important to get the full atmosphere and maintain an element of surprise. It's very entertaining for everyone else when somebody gets a soaking and they scream in shock, but do discourage them from leaping about too much or else they may fall down the steps or – even worse - topple overboard.

Cruising through tunnels can lead to optical illusions. While common sense tells you the surface of the canal must be level, much of the time you may be convinced that *Blissful Daze* is travelling up or down hill. Also tunnels never appear to be straight and some seem positively serpentine. This may not be a hallucination or the effect of too much booze, some tunnels do have decidedly wriggly lengths. It's the sections of bulging lining I find just a trifle worrying, especially where chunks of rock or brick look as though they may be about to drop on my head.

Other strange sensations you may experience in canal tunnels include thinking that: (1) The boat is sinking; (2) The far end of the tunnel is getting no nearer; and (3) Something has brushed through your hair. This may not have been your imagination; some tunnel roofs are low enough in places to concuss you; but then again it could be bats. Strangely, telling some boat crews that bats are often found in canal tunnels makes them less rather than more enthusiastic to enter one.

You can be sure that the headlamp of approaching boats will dazzle you. Although notionally adjustable, in reality they have been installed so, like the eyes of the Mona Lisa, wherever you go they always follow you. Another strange phenomenon you will notice inside tunnels is that all boat's headlamps are brighter than your own.

Blissful Daze may meet the occasional unseen object in your tunnel, such as floating barrels, sections of fencing, wooden doors (which give your crew a nasty jolt when they become wedged between the boat and the tunnel wall) or a broken-down boat without lights, in which case you will give its crew a nasty jolt if you don't spot them in time. Other occasional hazards include canoeists, workmen installing arrows that are supposed to glow in the dark, clouds of choking black smoke from other boat's chimney's, or in the Leeds & Liverpool Canal's Foulridge Tunnel, swimming cows.

Some canal tunnels are reputed to be haunted, like Crick, which boasts a ghastly female ghoul, and Harecastle, where you may meet the spectre of a woman wearing a bucket on her shoulders in place of her head, and called by the old boaters Kit Crewbucket. If you go into Blisworth Tunnel be sure to keep a good look out for the 'candlelit phantom fork'. This is supposed to appear at the spot where fourteen poor navvies who were digging out the tunnel died when the roof collapsed on them.

Saddington is another tunnel with its own spooky resident, while Saltersford Tunnel had such a bad reputation for phantoms that even the old boatmen were afraid to go through it alone. Nowadays we aren't frightened by such macabre anecdotes, are we? Come to think of it, perhaps your wriggly steering isn't due to lack of skill, some impish wraith could be to blame.

Over the years some ghastly and macabre happenings have taken place in the claustrophobic black depths of canal tunnels. Tales of asphyxiation and murder abound, but, for all that, navigating them is very exhilarating – though you may not fancy walking through any of the longer ones.

13 Overboard!

"If you have the misfortune of falling overboard it is best to walk to the side (but do it quickly) so no-one takes a photograph."
[**Hire Company Brochure.**]

As newcomers to canalling tend to find out in their first few hours afloat, all boating equipment has a mutinous determination to play truant at every opportunity. Whether it's your clothing, crockery, *Blissful Daze*'s ropes, life ring, boat hook, deck brush or the boarding plank, nothing wants to stay on board one minute longer than it can avoid. They may be blown off by the wind, get accidentally pushed over the side by your crew or casually vibrate in time with the throb of the engine until they slither overboard, but you can be sure everything will try its hardest to jump ship.

The moment you put your first mug of tea or coffee down on *Blissful Daze*'s roof, what will it do? Immediately slide off into the canal with a brief 'splish!' of relief. Spoons disappear even quicker. Leave your map laid out on the roof or deck without a selection of weights to restrain it, and before you can say "Gormless gongoozler!" the stupid thing will leap up in the air and flutter into the water, daring you to try to recover it. Canal guide books are just the same. On one trip I wrote out detailed plans for a revolutionary design of canal guide I called the Floating Companion. This would have been printed on waterproof paper and had its own built-in buoyancy aid and a tether to stop it escaping. What happened? All my notes blew overboard.

Newspapers, magazines, cameras, binoculars, books, glasses (both reading and drinking), packets of biscuits, sun tan lotion, mobile phones, cds, MP3 players etc., cans of beer, bottles of pop, children's toys and ladies' handbags. The list of items that have and will continue to hurl themselves off boats is endless. The only exceptions to this rule are the anchor, which spends all its time clipping your ankles, and that horror, the ghetto blaster. Unfortunately these seem capable of staying firmly attached to cabin tops in all conditions.

While she is firmly tied to the bank, it might seem unlikely, even in the dark, that anybody could fall off *Blissful Daze*; don't be too sure! If some dopey Dave or Dora forgets which side the towpath is, they could quickly find themselves trying, and failing, to walk on water. Then again, if your ropes are slackly tied or *Blissful Daze* comes adrift during your holiday – which by now you should accept as a near certainty – you may step across to where the bank ought to be, only to slither between it and your boat's hull. From this position the assistance of several strong and willing helpers may be required to pull you back on board. If this doesn't quite describe your shipmates, I suggest you take more care when stepping ashore.

Both leaving and returning to *Blissful Daze* will provide plenty of opportunities for falling in, especially if she is moored any distance from the bank. All those years ago up the Llangollen on *Woodstock,* this was the case at most of the places where we moored. Several times I thought myself particularly unlucky when, after making a dynamic leap ashore, the section of bank I'd landed on then crumbled under my weight and sent me slithering backwards into the water, wildly grasping handfuls of stinging nettles as I vainly tried to avoid another ducking. By the end of that first canal holiday my trousers had a tide mark just below the knees.

You may still make the mistake of selecting somewhere to moor which leaves *Blissful Daze* too far from the bank for your less agile crewmembers to straddle the gap. In such situations the obvious thing to do might seem to be to use the boarding plank, however, be warned, sometimes they only tend to make things worse. With *Blissful Daze*'s plank resting on a perfectly firm and solid-looking piece of ground, walking across should be as safe as houses, but if, as you reach the mid-point, *Smouldering Geyser* steams past, *Blissful Daze* will toss about and her plank will tip up, transforming you into a helpless cartwheeling airborne flurry of arms and legs before achieving splashdown.

Other things you should know about boarding planks are that they're awkward, sullen things that don't like being moved, and when roused they can be dangerous. If anyone asks you to grab the end as they swing a plank your way, **watch out !** You will most likely end up with a handful of splinters, get the villain dropped on your toes or find yourself pushed into the canal by it, or all three!

On a hot day it is common enough to see hire boat roofs littered with unoccupied crewmembers wearing the minimum of clothing, all sprawled on blankets, sleeping bags or duvets. It is almost as common, shortly after they pop below for a drink or to 'pump their bilges', now they are no longer acting as human pinions, for a mischievous gust of wind to cause their bedding to take on a life of its own. Believe me, it can lead to a fair level of confusion when an innocent steerer suddenly finds their head completely wrapped in a prickly blanket determined to suffocate them. Controlling the boat under these circumstances becomes quite impossible and some form of collision more or less inevitable.

Once you've heaved your sodden bedding out of the water, you'll be reminded that the drying facilities inside *Blissful Daze* weren't intended for anything larger than your underwear. Obviously the best place to put bulky items that need drying is back on the roof. When, or if, your laundry does dry out, it will probably then blow off the roof again! A good gust of wind can even blow your windlasses off the roof if you use them as weights. I'm not sure about your mallet, though. Try it and see.

As well as themselves and their bedding, hirers spread all sorts of items on their boat's roof in addition to the clutter of boating gear normally stored there. With low bridges and overhanging branches queuing up to sweep anything into the cut, this is just asking for trouble. Boat poles are probably the most lemming-like pieces of equipment. Most are round, and the moment you lay yours on *Blissful Daze*'s roof it will rush to the edge. Many hirers think the only reason their boat has rails along the roof edge is to stop their pole rolling off. Mind you, there are some boat owners who think their only purpose is to dangle masses of fenders from.

Some hire boat companies provide a metal equipment rack on the roof of their boats for storing the plank, poles and boathook, but as well as making sunbathing on the roof rather uncomfortable, these have a nasty knack of bruising your ankles and catching your toes every time you walk past. Tripping on them can be a very painful and spectacular way of diving into the canal. If you should do so, don't forget that usually there is no more than three feet of water, and half of that is liquid mud, so standing upside down in it is not to be recommended.

Although all the items on your boat's inventory will leap, roll or tumble overboard at every opportunity, crewmembers are even more prone to unintentionally parting company with their craft. Most boaters have their favourite stories about people falling in; almost invariably they concern someone else. While not wishing them any permanent harm or injury, you may, every now and then, hope that some particularly pompous canaller whom you've met will receive a ducking, preferably when you have a grandstand view and your camera at the ready. There are a variety of entertaining ways for other boaters to fall into the canal, as you will discover, given time.

Walking down those narrow, and often slippery, ledges along the cabin sides is tempting fate. On some boats these gunnels consist of a wicked obstacle course of cleats and eye fixings, all ever-ready to trip the unwary. Some even include a step just to increase the chances of hirers like you stubbing their toe and losing their footing.

Even without such hazards, if the gunnels or your feet are wet, it's on the cards that you will skid off whether *Blissful Daze* is moving or not. When this happens, if you manage to grab the handrail in time, it will provide an interesting test of your strength. Of course, if that wretched boat pole is in the way you've had it; as well as falling in the cut, you'll probably also break all your fingernails.

Once *Blissful Daze* gets under way, any of your crewmembers who take a fancy to whiling away the time perched on the roof will soon learn that this is the ideal place from which to carry out a survey of all the overhanging branches, overhead obstructions and low bridges along that stretch of the canal. They will also probably contribute to the boat colliding with something by blocking the view of the helmsman, as if the apprentice steerer didn't have enough trouble trying to keep control of their boat. Just remember to hold on tight.

Apart from minor scrapes, bumps and bashes, every now and again, *Blissful Daze* may come to a very abrupt and shuddering halt; like when she meets a large underwater obstruction – perhaps the roof of a stolen car or a ton of bricks – or, because her helmsman is so busy admiring the local talent, he steers her into the bank. When this happens, cries of anguish may be heard from below, particularly from anyone taking a shower or if the 'chef du jour' was wielding a sharp knife. The effect above decks may be even more dramatic. If, at the crucial moment, you were on lookout duty, perched on the bow like some over-sized figurehead, the parabola of your arc as you topple over *Blissful Daze*'s bow fender may appear quite graceful, unfortunately nothing else about your rapid disembarkation is likely to do so. Meanwhile, any idlers relaxing

The parabola of your arc as you topple over Blissful Daze's bow fender may appear quite graceful, unfortunately nothing else about your rapid disembarkation is likely to do so.

on the stern deck are also in danger of joining the ducks. Any crewmember perching on the stern rail will suddenly find themselves performing a rapid reverse somersault off the back of the boat. As for anybody standing on the roof, they'll fly so far they'll impress the local mallards!

Shipmates can, and frequently do, assist each other in parting company from their boat; so always keep a good lookout when any of them is wielding that boat pole or when they've finished using it. If they don't spot you standing behind them as they swing it across the roof and your head happens to be in the wrong place; OUCH!!. Such carelessness could result in the sound of wood hitting skull, shortly followed by that of a body hitting water, probably accompanied by a very loud yell, or two.

It will probably only take a day for you to realise that it can be a bad mistake to stand too close to the steerer. If they have to suddenly swing the tiller across to one side, as well as digging you painfully in the midriff, they could sweep you off the stern deck. Also try to appreciate that they won't be watching you, but the canal sixty or more feet ahead as they try to squeeze *Blissful Daze* into a lock or through a bridge hole. You can't expect them to ask you politely to move out of the way when they're desperately attempting to avoid colliding with *Smouldering Torrent* steaming towards you at a hundred miles an hour!

Children are particularly good at falling in and tend to do it at the most inconvenient moments. While Richard, a friend of mine, was concentrating on trying to wind up a Grand Union paddle a few years ago, one of his two young sons, Joe, without any warning, slipped off the side deck and disappeared beneath the surface of the water in the lock. Richard had never learned to swim, but thankfully he didn't need to go in, just managing to grab hold of Joe before he was totally full of water and then haul him back on board. This is one of the good things about young children, most are quite light. Imagine trying to heave a sodden twenty stone adult back on deck.

You'd never do it. That's a job that should only be attempted by professional weight-lifters, or with a crane.

And then there are the boat's ropes. As mentioned earlier, they're out to get you at every opportunity. So, as well as regularly tripping you up whenever you step ashore at your moorings, they will coil themselves around your ankles when *Blissful Daze* is on the move and do their best to send you sprawling. This may result in you flying down the back steps to collide with someone bringing out some steaming mugs of tea, crashing into the steerer so that he (or she) loses control and *Blissful Daze* abruptly changes course and thumps into *Tranquil Waters*, or leaves you a clear path to shoot headlong over the side and an opportunity to sample the quality of the local canal water. Don't worry, it isn't polluted everywhere.

There is also just a slight chance of one or more of the adults on *Blissful Daze* falling off her as a result of drinking too much alcohol. Hire company brochures boast about the attractions of canalside pubs and all the cruising guides tell innocent boaters about all the hostelries along their route that shouldn't be missed. So, if once in a while, *Blissful Daze*'s skipper, on finding a handy mooring place around midday, ties up outside *The Romping Tortoise* or *The Beetle and Barge Pole*, her crew shouldn't be blamed for checking out the quality of the beer on sale.

It is when they get back on board with several pints inside them that accidents may happen. Inebriated steerers are a menace to all other boaters and should be relieved of the helm without delay. Sozzled crewmembers may also need to be discouraged from frolicking on the roof or tap-dancing down the gunnel, but the classic scene is surely when a tiddly canaller helps to push off the bow with one foot on the boat while the other is still anchored to the bank. When he finds the gap is too great for him to get on board or retreat to dry land and can do the splits no longer, he has no choice but to plummet into the water between the two. Such performances bring great delight to the watching gongoozlers and instant embarrassment, pain and sobriety to the victim.

As well as all the accidental ways of falling overboard, there's just a chance that before your cruise is over your crew may decide the most effective way for them to express their appreciation of your captaincy of *Blissful Daze* is to throw you off her. Just pray they don't tie the anchor to your ankles.

Taking an impromptu ducking is all part and parcel of the total canalling experience, so don't be worried or embarrassed when you fall overboard. You'll laugh about it later. I have just two pieces of advice for anyone who falls in: Have some dry clothes to change into and don't stay under too long.

14 *Back to base.*

"Hirers must allow margins for delays and will,
at the Company's discretion, be held liable for late return."
[**Hire Company Brochure.**]

DESPITE appearing so cramped when you first boarded her, I'll bet *Blissful Daze*'s cabins seemed to expand as you got used to them and to working round each other. At times it may have been 'moving by numbers', but you all soon found your own favourite perch or corner.

By the time we reached Llangollen town, Bill had knocked us into a capable crew. Max and I had become pretty good at leaping back on board after closing lock gates behind *Woodstock* as she steamed out of them with Bill at the helm. If the truth be told, not all his manoeuvres were completely successful and it wasn't unknown for the hulls of boats we met to thump, bash, grind and scrape alongside *Woodstock*'s as we passed. When this happened Bill would give their steerer one of his most disdainful scowls until they apologised, when, relenting, he would treat them to a charming smile and forgivingly call out "Think nothing of it."

Resourceful hirers who discover shortcomings in their boat's inventory, such as the absence of fenders, may quickly come up with a D-I-Y solution. We found the noise of *Woodstock*'s hull grating against the concrete edges hard to bear and fished some old tyres out of the water (that's what the boathook is there for!) and hung them from the handrails with bits of rope we'd salvaged from the weed hatch. After seeing a hirer on this canal busily threading some string through his boat's doormat for the same reason, I began to wonder what other solutions there might be to this problem. Perhaps you could wrap a pillow in a bin liner, if someone is prepared to give up their pillow, or, as a last resort, why not get one of those bloated animal corpses you see floating in the cut and tie it alongside. Maybe that's not such a good idea. It could be rather unpleasant in hot weather!

During your week you're bound to need to exercise some ingenuity now and again to overcome the little challenges that canal cruising always throws up. If one night Dick Dastardly's boat charges past wrenching *Blissful Daze*'s mooring pins out of the bank, you will have plenty of reasons to curse the inconsiderate steerer. Your thoughts as you struggle to pole your boat back to the bank will be as nothing to those when you realise that your only mooring pins have been swallowed up by the canal. Now what are you going to tie to? Put on your thinking cap, and while you're at it, also remember to put on some shoes before going ashore. You should have learned by now that canal towpaths have more than their fair share of nettles, thistles and discarded cans and bottles, as well as being very popular with dogs!

You won't need any help from other boaters to lose your mooring pins, or mallet, windlasses or any other piece of equipment for that matter. You'll manage perfectly well on your own. Whether it's dropping them in the water or leaving them behind at locks and mooring places. Before your week is through and you return *Blissful Daze* to her boatyard, you can be sure that some (if not all) of this equipment will have disappeared. If this happens in mid-week, just getting her back to Blissful Boats' hire base may prove an interesting test of your initiative.

When some 'Careless Charlie' leaves a windlass behind at a lock, it is rarely worth going back to look for it. They mysteriously vanish into thin air in next to no time. Forget to put your pins or mallet back on board when leaving a mooring and, pound to a penny, by the time you realise and send someone running back down the towpath to retrieve them, they will have evaporated. However, if you drop things into the canal, you do stand a chance of getting them back: although only a slim one! A keen skipper may immediately insist on everyone (except themselves) grappling with the boat hook and, if necessary, wading about in the water until the lost piece of equipment is recovered. But after the first ten minutes the novelty of the search will probably wear off and then the crew will vote to abandon it. Otherwise they won't reach the next watering hole.

Banging in mooring pins without the mallet calls for more improvisation and should be attempted by the bonehead responsible for losing it. This will teach them to be more careful in future. If *Blissful Daze* started out with two windlasses, the loss of one shouldn't be a problem, although it is likely to slow your progress through locks when everybody squabbles over whose turn it is to use the 'winding thingummyjig'. Lose all your windlasses though, and you may have to revise your plans rather drastically unless you can replace them.

Inexperienced crews can often be seen with their lines secured around the rail on a section of piled bank, but it won't be long before the sharp edges of the metal gnaw at and fray them until they look like a cat's tail that has been blow-dried. Perhaps *Blissful Daze*'s ropes were like that when you took her over; if so, you know how they got that way.

If you don't mind revealing your stupidity at losing vital pieces of equipment to a succession of strangers, you can try asking fellow boaters for assistance. They will probably enjoy giving you advice and may even help you through locks, but the only boating paraphernalia they're likely to give you are the miserable, misshapen items they were thinking of chucking out anyway. Obviously other hire boaters won't have any spare items, they'll be short of things themselves! You may be fortunate and locate a convenient boatyard where you can buy new gear quite soon, but, then again you may not; in which case you'll have to keep on improvising for the remainder of your cruise.

As the days pass, the crew of *Blissful Daze* may become more observant and start to notice some of the interesting examples of industrial archaeology on the canal. For instance, at some locks those wooden planks on the top gates that rookies nervously sidle across, have intriguing indentations, while above them are some weirdlyshaped handrails. In time you will work out how these happened, unless you already know because your boat was responsible for them in the first place! What is more of a mystery is how there come to be large chunks of masonry missing from some bridge arches round about head height.

On some boats the helmsman's view seems to be completely blocked by the rest of his crew. Should you have this problem one day when you're on the tiller, if the trees are wet with dew or from an earlier shower, there's a great opportunity to extract your revenge by steering through the lowest overhanging branches. To avoid being lynched you may need a good excuse, such as having to manoeuvre past an approaching boat. Failing this, you could always invent an imaginary swarm of wasps you had to avoid, or blame that old standby, the wind. They may just believe you!

Try using your canal guide in the rain and you will discover that they tend to smudge. If yours has already taken a dip or two it will be pretty hard to decipher even in dry conditions. So let's hope you don't arrive at any junctions in a downpour, as getting any of your crew to come out of the nice dry cabin to help decide which way to go will not be easy. While you're still summoning assistance, *Blissful*

Daze will continue drifting forward and most likely collide with either the bank or another boat, or both.

There's always plenty to look at as your boat meanders along her watery route, and once you've learned to steer a straightish line when passing moored craft, you can have a good laugh at the names some people have given their boats. It's hard not to wonder who named their boat *Pig in Shades* or *Watership Up; Slow Mo Shun* or *Appydaze*; *Weir Lost ll* or *Knackered Navvy*. Yes, they're all genuine names I've spotted. At least *Flat Bottom Girl* makes sense, *Narrow Escape* is very appropriate and *Karma Waters* rather clever, while *Bacon Butty*, *A Nonny Mouse* and *Minced Moorhen* raise a chuckle. But my favourite has to be *Comedy of Errors*.

As your holiday nears its end, perhaps your crew will finally cure themselves of the habit of placing their drinks on the roof, not least because, after losing several of the boat's original mugs and breaking the rest, you bought a new set from a canalside shop. Which sort did you choose, those decorated with roses and castles? Or ones painted with 'Skipper', 'Crew', 'Mate' and 'Galley Slave'? Don't bother to buy a lace plate for a fussy relative who doesn't understand about them. They'll only complain "That plate you bought me, dear, was no good, it was full of holes. I should take it back and get a refund!"

You might think (or at least hope) that the on-board catering will improve as people begin to get to grips with the limitations of *Blissful Daze*'s galley. This is most unlikely. Your most competent cook will probably volunteer (I use the term loosely) to prepare meals at the start of the trip and will use up all the best ingredients by the time they resign. It will now fall to someone else to take over the apron. When your second choice cook was anxious to find a successor, (probably within twenty-minutes!), they may have reckoned their best ploy was to produce something utterly disgusting, or burnt, or, just to be sure of being barred from any more cooking, disgusting <u>and</u> burnt. Did you bring any indigestion tablets?

Instead of having one cook, some crews spread the load and everyone has a go. This is much fairer, but doesn't tend to improve either the quality or variety of the catering. What you can be sure of is that every night on the canals lots of boaters are sitting down to 'bangers and beans'.

Towards the end of your trip, supper may consist of rather unusual concoctions where the ingredients could include any or all of the following: eggs, sardines, mashed potato, tinned tomatoes, tinned peas, stewed steak, spaghetti, baked beans and pickle. Unrepeatable mixtures of food are a typical feature of that final evening on any boating trip, but if you have planned things well, there will be a reasonable pub within staggering distance where this meal can be quickly forgotten about. If you can afford it, why not avoid the hassle of cooking and washing up by treating your stomachs to supper at the pub. With luck, by the end of the evening everyone will be convinced they have really enjoyed their canal holiday. Pay for all their drinks and your crew may even agree that you've been a good skipper.

As well as celebrating the success of your cruise, you may treat yourself to an extra glass to keep from thinking about a certain nasty moment that can't be avoided in the morning. Someone will have to report the return of *Blissful Daze* to the boatyard and own up to Blissful Boats certain damage she has sustained, as well as explaining any breakages, lost equipment and why there is now a large knot joining the two pieces of her stern rope. Guess who that someone is!

On your final morning the scene inside *Blissful Daze* will be even more chaotic than any time previously (which is saying something!) as everyone frantically searches for their belongings while trying to tidy up their bedding, remove the gravy, ketchup, squash, tea, coffee, salad cream and jam stains and generally make an effort to leave the boat in a reasonable condition.

There seem to be three schools of thought on where to moor on your final evening. Some crews like to be right outside the boatyard to save hurrying in the morning, while others prefer to leave a couple of hours cruising so as to spin out their holiday as much as possible. The third don't mind where they moor just so long as its close to a good pub. We had to get back from Llangollen on our final morning, but with the flow behind us, *Woodstock* sped down the cut and we arrived with minutes to spare, 'a triumph of navigation', well that's what I thought!

You may have a lump in your throat or give a heartfelt sigh of relief as *Blissful Daze* comes alongside at the boatyard and you reach journey's end. Either way, please try not to ram any of the other boats tied up on the wharf. Now it's time to report to the office. Grit your teeth and 'go for it'.

Unless you are an exceptional crew, the boatyard staff will be remarkably unfazed by your list of damaged and lost items. Burnt out kettles, collapsed bunks, singed carpets, cracked windows, broken shafts and planks, bent cleats and mangled ropes. They've seen it all before, and, incredibly, there are many hirers much worse than your bunch. Some boats have been returned completely wrecked, and some craft haven't been returned at all, when their hirers got so bored with working all those locks that they just abandoned their boat miles from its base. Now that, I imagine, does upset the boatyard manager.

You've spent the week travelling at a snail's pace in a previous century and somehow everyone has got on throughout the holiday – most of the time anyway. As you say goodbye to *Blissful Daze* it occurs to you all that your introduction to canalling has been just what a holiday is supposed to be, 'a break'. During the week, one way and another, you have probably broken quite a few things, but in the process you've enjoyed some novel experiences, laughed a lot and even learnt a bit about boating and canals.

Now it is time to return to the real world, and the real world is a much faster moving and less friendly place than the cut. Never mind, you've a store of happy memories, all those films to be developed, and it's not completely beyond the bounds of possibility that you might go on a canal holiday again; stranger things have been known.

15 Caught on film.

"Our feet were undoubtedly the leading article in that photograph. Indeed very little else was to be seen."
[**Three Men in a Boat** by Jerome K. Jerome.]

Most of us own a camera, whether it's one of those supermarket use-once-and-throw-away types, built into your mobile phone or a top-of-the-range camcorder or digital model with all the buttons and gizmos designed to keep the 'Got-to-haves' three steps ahead of the Joneses.

During your first week's boating there will be almost too many hilarious moments to do justice to, but, whatever your snaps or videos turn out like, taking them will add an extra dimension to your canal trip, and looking at them after you return home will help everyone relive the highs and lows of your canal holiday.

When Selina and Max pushed us away from the wharf, Bill took *Woodstock's* helm and I grabbed my camera to capture the scene as we sedately chugged across the daunting Pontcysyllte Aqueduct. I still treasure those photos of Bill, pipe clenched firmly between his teeth and eyes sparkling with pleasure, looking like an admiral posing for his portrait. Jillie, by contrast, appears rather less confident, gazing apprehensively at the awful drop on either side of the boat and gripping the handrail as though her life depended on it.

All my snapshots show Max being busy, whether standing at the bow, with raised boat hook, ready to jump into action at any moment, or experimenting with using the boarding plank as a seat across the stern rails. He persevered with this idea until the splinters got the better of him! But he never could sit still.

It's not easy taking good 'action shots' on the canals. For instance when you snap away as one of the wrinklies pushes on a balance beam, you may not realise what a prominent feature her sizeable backside will be in the resulting photo. Two small children gamely pushing the same gate open is a charming sight, but your print will do less than justice to it when everything except the tops of their heads and four sets of fingers is obscured by the bulk of the balance beam.

I hardly clicked my camera at the locks, not because I didn't want to, but because before I could peer through the viewfinder, someone always bawled instructions to wind a paddle or push a gate. Only my young nephew had a lazy time at locks.

My attempts at using the flash inside tunnels proved a total waste of film. Like some of my other efforts, they came out so fuzzy or dark that nobody has ever been able to make out what the original subject was.

Having a good camera and a sober operator may help, but to get the fullest coverage of your exploits, I reckon you need a spare crewmember (you thought they were all spare!). Why not give someone the sole task of recording all those little incidents that add so much spice and excitement to your boating activities? Like when Grandad dropped the mallet on his foot and hopped around trying to clutch it, until he fell over the mooring rope and landed in a clump of nettles. There were tears in his eyes, poor man; just the memory of it will bring tears of laughter to your own.

There were tears in his eyes, poor man.

There may be problems if nobody wants to be the official photographer, in which case pick the member of your crew who is least use at the locks, a hard choice perhaps! But more likely everyone will volunteer. The fairest system would be to draw up a rota, or you could do what most crews do and let the first person to grab the camera and leap ashore do the snapping. Just so long as somebody keeps the shutter clicking.

Unfortunately we didn't think to assign anyone to film our magic moments, so we have no souvenirs of *Woodstock* getting stuck on the mud or ramming the bank, nor of our confusion at the Grindley Brook staircase or of Max falling in. We could have given the camera to Jillie, but then we'd have ended up with nothing but pictures of baby Guy!

For your own satisfaction I suggest you try to make yours a more complete record. If you have a camera with a zoom lens, you'll be able to capture, for all time, the looks of disbelief and terror on the faces of the people sitting at the front of other boats as *Blissful Daze* bears down on them at speed, and a collision seems inevitable. Then be sure to keep filming when the crunch comes (try not to be thrown overboard) and don't stop until you've caught that marvellous shot of the passing crew shaking their fists at your steerer. Happy memories.

When *Blissful Daze* runs aground, provided no-one beats you to it, and you can jump that far, be the first to volunteer to leap ashore, taking the camera with you of course. How everyone will laugh in months and years to come when they look at your photos showing all of them struggling to grab hold of the boat pole and fighting to extricate themselves from a tangle of overhanging branches. And if you successfully photograph anybody actually falling in, you will have a picture to be proud of for ever and a day.

Children will also enjoy collecting never-to-be forgotten snaps of their boating holiday; like Dad's face turning a bright shade of purple as he struggles to raise a paddle rather stiffer than the average, or the scene as one of the marooned crinklies tries for the fourth time to throw a, by now, decidedly wet rope from the drifting boat to the rest of *Blissful Daze*'s crew stranded on the bank.

The classic photograph must result when everyone huddles together on the stern for a group shot, and finding they won't all quite fit into the viewfinder, the photographer moves back one step too far and, with a screech of surprise and horror, plummets into the water while desperately holding the camera aloft. The result, provided the camera survives, may be a fine, but strangely angled, shot of the sky. Perhaps I ought to have included the suggestion that you only take *waterproof* cameras on your canal holiday. There are some people who certainly should!

Missing part (or even all) of your intended subject will probably be less of a problem if you swap your Brownie Quickshot for a camcorder. Even if you're no Stephen Spielberg, you should get some entertaining material as you scan from one end of *Blissful Daze* to the other. It may be best to warn your crew when you are about to film them, otherwise they might find themselves videoed doing something embarrassing just as your lens captures them in the act. On second thoughts, no, don't warn them.

Video too must be far better at preserving for posterity in agonising detail the complete incompetence of some crews to work in unison. It would be a crime not to record the chaos when half of her crew are attempting to work *Blissful Daze* through a lock while the other half are intent on mooring her up and going to the nearby pub for lunch, or how your skipper reacts when he unexpectedly spots the bow of a boat nosing through a bridge only yards ahead.

It isn't only your own antics that should be filmed. Other boaters will provide wonderful photographic opportunities every day. Take for example this classic scene down at Hurleston. At the same time that a boat was exiting the bottom lock and making for the nearby T-junction, two boats were travelling towards the bridge which crosses the main line there, one going north and the other heading south. All three helmsmen appeared unaware of the other two craft and continued to converge on the same spot. By the time the first of them realised the situation, it was too late to do much other than throw the throttle into reverse and cross their fingers. To do that scene of carnage full justice, as well as capturing the slewing boats, clouds of exhaust smoke and frantically gesticulating figures, it would have been essential to record the sound of crunching metal, splintering glass and the shrieks of terror from the people caught in the centre of this classic pile up.

Watch out that your camera or camcorder doesn't fall into the wrong hands. You could find it short of film or drained of power after some poetical individual has shot off hundreds of whimsical portraits of cloud formations or clumps of thistles, or if a teenager in your crew decides to make a thorough catalogue of all the passing talent.

Looking at your photos for the first time, you will almost certainly be surprised at how many feature *Blissful Daze*'s roof. When you pressed the button you were intent on getting good portraits of your shipmates or children, but they appear in the middle distance, while dominating every scene are thirty feet of boat's roof complete with mop, plank, boat hook and her mud-splattered pole.

A photo of that same roof taken at very close quarters may puzzle everyone for a bit, until they realise that the individual taking it was so intent on recording the antics of everybody on the stern that they failed to spot a large branch approaching them from the rear.

We haven't got any photos of *Woodstock*'s interior, perhaps it was always too untidy, but I have noticed that adults always seem embarrassed at being snapped inside a boat, even when they're fully clothed. So take plenty of shots inside as well as out, but be ready for your victims to turn the tables on you.

One problem you might experience is in trying to agree exactly where and when certain photos were taken. Heated arguments may flare up with competing claims for each shot. "That's the place where you dropped our last windlass in the water." "No, it isn't; it's where we stayed tied up for three hours waiting for you to come back from buying some ice cream." "You're both wrong. I took it just after we found we'd moored next to that wasp's nest. That's why we're all waving our arms about." It doesn't really matter that you can't agree on the details; just looking at your photos is bound to stir up a mixture of memories and emotions.

Yes, during the long winter months you can always cheer yourself up by getting out your videos or album and reliving the extraordinary catalogue of experiences on your first canal holiday. Remember the characters you met, the pubs you tried to drink dry, the relief once you had successfully crossed those aqueducts, the nervous tension inside the tunnels and your partner's glow of pride (and your surprise) when they successfully slid *Blissful Daze* into a lock without touching the sides.

Your films will become a priceless memento of a unique adventure and something to cherish, for, however often you go canalling again, there will never be anything quite like that first magic time when you fell under the spell, and come what may, you will never forget your week spent on *Blissful Daze*.

The seed, once sown, will grow despite any attempts to blight it. No use saying "But everyone quarrelled all the time and then blamed me when we got hopelessly lost." or "Half the crew got food poisoning." or even "We spent most of the time in a drunken stupor, bumping into other boats, banks and lock sides."

What does it matter that you miscalculated how long the trip would take and had to begin the last three days at five o'clock each morning, almost sank a work boat in the lock, and that the headlight fused and you had to creep through that tunnel with everyone striking matches!

Time is a wonderful healer. With your bruises forgotten, you will recall those minor mishaps on your holiday with a grin and a chuckle at how unprepared you all were. Before you realise what is happening, you'll begin to feel restless to get back to the cut. Why you're even starting to talk like a real boater.

If you were to go canal cruising again, you wouldn't be a greenhorn any more. Compared to the next crop of first timers you'd be quite an old hand, able to offer the occasional word of advice to those unseasoned novices and to show them how things ought to be done. Those boats from the Easy Boating Company looked well-equipped and nicely turned out. What is their website address?

I'm afraid you are hooked, but don't worry, you will never be an L-driver again. Now you know your puddle from your paddle and what gear to bring on board and what to leave behind. Following your inauguration into the select world of those who have survived a holiday on the canals, next time (with your camera poised) you will be ready to enjoy to the full both your own canalling and other boaters' skill and occasional lack of it!